THE LAST
CAVALRYMAN

Dedicated to the memory of Harry Holgate (1908-1994).
A good man, and the best Dad anyone could wish for.
Also, to Julia Elisabeth Wigley (1938-2024) his "Little Sweetheart."

With thanks to Sue Fryer for her help and encouragement.

THE LAST CAVALRYMAN

Memoirs of a British Dragoon 1927–1944

ROGER HOLGATE

Pen & Sword
MILITARY

AN IMPRINT OF PEN & SWORD BOOKS LTD.
YORKSHIRE – PHILADELPHIA

First published in Great Britain in 2025 by
Pen & Sword Military
An imprint of
Pen & Sword Books Ltd
Yorkshire – Philadelphia

Copyright © Roger Holgate, 2025

ISBN 978 1 03613 018 3

The right of Roger Holgate to be identified as the Author of this work has been asserted by him in accordance with the Copyright, Designs and Patents Act 1988.

A CIP catalogue record for this book is available from the British Library.

All rights reserved. No part of this book may be reproduced, transmitted, downloaded, decompiled or reverse engineered in any form or by any means, electronic or mechanical including photocopying, recording or by any information storage and retrieval system, without permission from the Publisher in writing. NO AI TRAINING: Without in any way limiting the Author's and Publisher's exclusive rights under copyright, any use of this publication to "train" generative artificial intelligence (AI) technologies to generate text is expressly prohibited. The Author and Publisher reserve all rights to license uses of this work for generative AI training and development of machine learning language models.

Typeset by SJmagic DESIGN SERVICES, India.

Printed and bound in the UK by CPI Group (UK) Ltd.

The Publisher's authorised representative in the EU for product safety is Authorised Rep Compliance Ltd., Ground Floor, 71 Lower Baggot Street, Dublin D02 P593, Ireland.
www.arccompliance.com

For a complete list of Pen & Sword titles please contact

PEN & SWORD BOOKS LIMITED
George House, Units 12 & 13, Beevor Street, Off Pontefract Road,
Barnsley, South Yorkshire, S71 1HN, England
E-mail: enquiries@pen-and-sword.co.uk
Website: www.pen-and-sword.co.uk

or

PEN AND SWORD BOOKS
1950 Lawrence Rd, Havertown, PA 19083, USA
E-mail: uspen-and-sword@casematepublishers.com
Website: www.penandswordbooks.com

Contents

Illustrations vii
Maps x
Preface xi
Prologue xiii

Session 1	The Hussars	1
Session 2	Cavalry Training	5
Session 3	Afridi Campaign	12
Session 4	Sheep's Eyeballs and a Scuttled Ship	20
Session 5	Ghandi, an Air Crash, and the Punkah Wallah	34
Session 6	On the Road to Damascus	42
Session 7	Peace and War	46
Session 8	The Last Cavalryman	50
Session 9	A Mysterious Compound and the Ford 6-Tonners	61
Session 10	Secrets and Lies	65
Session 11	El Alamein	73
Session 12	A Chat with the Enemy	86
Session 13	The Casualty Clearing Station	90
Session 14	Wide-eyed and Almost Legless	94
Session 15	Via Dolorosa	96
Session 16	Hear All, See All, Say Nowt	101

Session 17	The Left Hook	104
Session 18	A Wildcat and a Stranded Whale	122
Session 19	Artillery Spotter for the Yanks, and the Bouncing Betties	129
Session 20	The Anzio Runs and Other Eruptions	132
Session 21	The Caesar Line, a Trip to Rome, and a Pig	139
Session 22	Florence, Morpeth, and Home	152
Appendix I	Message from Commander of British Eighth Army	154
Appendix II	Message from General H R Alexander to Commanding Officer Queen's Own Yorkshire Dragoons	156
Appendix III	Army Form of Attestation	157
Appendix IV	Certificate of Service	159
Appendix V	Certificate of Transfer to Army Reserve	162
Appendix VI	Certificate of Discharge	163
Appendix VII	Educational Attainments, Trade Qualifications, Medals	164
Appendix VIII	Soldier's Service Book	165
Appendix IX	Newspaper Article 28th July 1941	173
Appendix X	Record of Service	175
Appendix XI	Standing Orders for Drivers	176
Appendix XII	Character Reference	177
Appendix XIII	World War Two Identification Tags	178
Appendix XIV	Service Medals	179
Appendix XV	Dried flowers postcard to Julie, sent from Uncle Addy, Jerusalem, November 1942	180
Glossary		181
Remembrance		189

Illustrations

1. Boer War Mounted Yeomanry xiv
2. Troopers "Polly" Perkins, and "Muchie" Poole. Fulford Barracks, York, 1927 2
3. Tent pegging 3
4. Cavalry Trooper in marching order 7
5. Lee-Enfield SMLE Mk. III 10
6. Cavalry charge from "Balaclava" 13
7. British Indian Army soldiers in Peshawar, 1930 16
8. A group of Afridi warriors 18
9. HMAS Vampire and HMAS Voyager encrusted with ice. Marseilles harbour, 1940 26
10. Sergeant Harry Holgate, the Plains of Esdraelon, Palestine, 1940 28
11. A tribal lunch at a cavalry post at Tel-el-Meleiha 20 miles North of Beersheeba, 18th January 1940 29
12. View of Haifa Bay from Mount Carmel 30
13. Ghandi at a protest meeting, Peshawar, North-West Frontier 34
14. Hawker Hart 36
15. British mounted troops, Syria 1941 43
16. With Flash, Ezraa, Syria, July 1941 45

17. "The Flying Scotsman" under repair at Doncaster Railway Works 1922 46
18. Australian Walers 48
19. Tell Qeni, the highest mountain in the Jabal-al-Druze 51
20. Bedford Lorry in the Western Desert, 1941 62
21. Ford 6-tonne Prime Mover Lorry..63
22. The framework of a dummy tank under construction at the Middle East School of Camouflage in the Western Desert, 1942 66
23. A Stuart tank being refuelled from a fuel bowser outside Sidi Barrani, 15th November 1942 69
24. An RAF Lysander flies over a convoy of lorries during the retreat into Egypt, 26th June 1942 70
25. Yorkshire Dragoons, Cairo, 1941..75
26. A 25-pdr gun firing during the British night artillery barrage which opened the Second Battle of El Alamein, 23rd October 1942 76
27. In the minefield, El Alamein, October 1942 78
28. A British soldier inspects the grave of a German tank crewman, killed when his PzKpfw III tank was knocked out in the Western Desert, 29th September 1942 80
29. British tanks move up to engage the German armour after the infantry had cleared gaps in the enemy minefield, El Alamein, 24th October 1942...85
30. German prisoners of the 90th Light Infantry Division, El Alamein, 1942..87
31. A British soldier gives the "insult" version of a V-for-Victory sign to German prisoners from the 90th Light Infantry Division, El Alamein, 1942..88
32. Captured Stuka dive bomber, North Africa, 1941.......................91

Illustrations

33. A British Army doctor examines patients at a Casualty Clearing Station in Tunisia, February 1943 92
34. Old City of Jerusalem 97
35. Yorkshire Dragoons, Alexandria, 1942 98
36. The leader of an RAF transport convoy bound for Tunisia, signals his vehicles to move off from their base in Libya, 1943 102
37. Crusader tanks at El Hamma, 29th March 1943 110
38. Landing ships unloading supplies in Anzio harbour, 19th – 24th February 1944 123
39. Anzio Beachhead, 1944 124
40. US Sherman tanks disembarking from an LST, Anzio, 1944 126
41. Anzio, 1940. Lavinio can be seen at the far end of the beach 128
42. British infantry occupies a captured German communications trench during the offensive at Anzio, 22nd May 1944 130
43. A British soldier guards German prisoners, Anzio 1944 133
44. Mt. Vesuvius erupts, March 1944 134
45. PIAT in action, 1944 141
46. Allied troops in Rome, June 1944 143
47. The author, with the Nazi flag that his father took from a German tank at Anzio, 1944 148
48. Party for the families of serving Dragoons, Danum Ballroom, Doncaster, January 1944 151
49. Doncaster Railway Station, September 1944. Left to right: Julie, Kit, Mary, Pat, Harry, and Carroll 153

Maps

North-West Frontier of India in 1930 15
Marseilles and surrounding area 21
Syria, Palestine, Lebanon, Transjordan, 1941 44
The Western Desert, 1942 74
Outflanking The Mareth Line, 19th – 28th March 1943 106
The Breakout from Anzio, 23rd – 24th May 1944 140

Preface

Dad was in his seventies when I finally got him to sit down and talk about his experiences in the army. He'd told me the odd tale or two before this, but they were few and far between and I had difficulty in putting them in chronological order. When we were both younger it didn't seem to matter that he had some important bits of history in his head, but as time went on, I started to realize that if I was going to record this history I would have to start soon. That's when I nagged him into giving me a series of interviews and pushed and questioned him all the way through. He was still as sharp as a button, as he used to say, and when I got out the maps of desert battles, and the letters from home, they stirred some remarkably vivid memories of places, dates, incidents, and people.

The stories in this book reflect my father's recollection of events. Although the characters involved were indeed real, I have changed the names of several of those depicted, in order to protect their privacy, and that of their families.

Roger Holgate

"God forbid that I should go to any Heaven in which there are no horses."

Robert Bontine Cunninghame Graham (1852-1936), adventurer, politician, journalist, and writer.

Prologue

I joined the army in 1927. There wasn't much else around at that time, jobwise, and anyway, I fancied getting out of Hunslet and seeing a bit of the world. I didn't reckon on seeing quite as much of it as I ended up doing, but that was all down to fate, I suppose, and none of us know our fate. I'm grateful for that when I recall all the blokes that died alongside me. It was always better not to know in advance, I'm sure.

I started out as a hussar; that was on account of how I wanted to be a horse soldier and they sounded good enough to me.

Hussars were supposed to be light cavalry, and to start with they had only their swords to do the fighting with. By the time I joined they had changed quite a bit and had rifles and machine gun detachments, but they allus regarded themselves as a cut above the dragoons, who were supposed to be just infantry on horses.

I ended up being a dragoon and I found out that the word came from the old matchlock guns that they used donkey's years ago. Apparently, when they got fired, they used to throw out sparks and smoke, like a dragon's supposed to do. Anyroad, they started decorating the things with engravings of dragons, and that's where the dragoons got their name. Least, that's what they told me.

The Queen's Own Yorkshire Dragoons was my regiment, and they'd fought in the Boer War as yeomanry: a sort of volunteer, part-time soldier.

After that, they fought in the First World War, not generally on horseback because they found out that horses don't last long when they charge at machine guns. Having said that, they did do a lot of mounted reconnaissance work on those occasions when they weren't needed to support the infantry with their heavy machine guns. In the end, they started running out of horses and the stuff to feed them, so the Yorkshire Dragoons became cyclists, riding about with messages and the like.

1. Boer War Mounted Yeomanry. Skeoch Cumming W (1864–1929). (Wikimedia Commons)

After the war, the dragoon's headquarters were moved to a barracks in Danum Road, Doncaster, and when I left the regular army in 1933, I signed up as a territorial with them (that was a part-time soldier you know). I was a musketry instructor, and I allus thought of mesen as a dragoon, after that.

Anyroad, that's where I was when Hitler decided to invade Poland on 3rd September 1939.

SESSION 1

The Hussars

I remember fretting about the water bucket. It's funny what you fret about at times like that, but it was leaking, and I was thinking that Flash would need it before we were done. I remember the engine jerking forrard and me leaning out the window again and holding your mum's hand, and I can remember that bucket but not what she said to me. Funny innit? I think I said summat to her about looking after the bairns, although I knew she would, and some other drivel about seeing her soon, though I had no way of knowing if that were true, or not. But I said it anyway, as the train began to move out and the platform clock ticked round to midnight. I remember that too, on account of it was 1940.

We were heading for France. Not that they told us, but you didn't need much gumption to work it out. The Germans were still laiking about on the French border and the general opinion seemed to be that they were in two minds about attacking. But we were going there, anyway.

I climbed over a wooden partition, into Flash's stall, and sat on a bale of hay so I could stroke his face. By 'eck, he was a bobby-dazzler was Flash. He shoved his nose into mine and I could smell the hay on his breath, and I remembered the first time I'd been in a stable, 1927 that was. Fulford Barracks, York, and Troop Sergeant Drew standing in the doorway as I went in and stood there gawping at a beautiful chestnut mare. She'd nudged me for the carrot I was holding, and I'd given it her, and I remember Sergeant Drew saying, "this is Rosie. Alright for you lad?" and me saying "champion sarge."

By God that was a great time in my life!

I'd only joined up after getting made redundant from Mr Shoot's shop in Leeds, where I'd been an apprentice tailor, you know. Anyroad, I joined the army, and they gave me the number, 547113, and then I did my basic training in Canterbury: drill, kit cleaning, and the like. I'd never been out of Leeds before, and Canterbury was a different world. We often went to town, me and my mate Ben Widdowson, dressed in our khakis and feeling like the bee's knees and chatting up all the lasses. I remember the jammy bugger got off with a reight little cracker from Faversham. We had some good times, me and Ben.

One day, they called us all in and told us what units we could volunteer for. I said the cavalry because I'd always liked horses, though I'd only seen them at the pictures and when I'd been helping Mr Hawkswell with his milk deliveries. He used to let me ride Dora when she was pulling his milk cart. The sergeant said I could choose from the King's Dragoon Guards, the 11th Hussars, or the 14/20th Hussars. and as I was getting addled by all the names, and hadn't a clue about any of them, I told him I'd have the last one. He looked at me as if I was barmy.

Ben came with me to Fulford and got posted to 3rd Troop, B Squadron. I got 1st Troop. That's when I first met Troop Sergeant Drew, who looked like a jockey and cursed like a sailor. He was alright though, and he soon took an interest in my riding skills and said he thought I was a natural. I must admit that I fell off more times than Soft Mick, but I suppose that was only to be expected, and it was grand to be out there with Rosie every

2. Troopers "Polly" Perkins, and "Muchie" Poole, Fulford Barracks, York, 1927. Unknown. (© Roger Holgate)

3. Tent pegging. Unknown. (Wikimedia Commons)

day. At first, I suppose I was a bit cack-handed with everything and Rosie could be a bit of a barmpot, but we learned together, the two of us. Well, we must've done, because I got picked as recruit of the year and got presented with a riding crop that had the regimental crest on it. Wish I still had it, but it disappeared somewhere in India.

Anyroad, I got picked to represent the regiment in the Aldershot Tattoo army horse trials at Rushmore Arena and Sergeant Drew lent me his own horse, Sadie. She was smaller than Rosie and just right for tent pegging. He was the sergeant in the three-man team and Major Darley was the officer. He was from the Darley family in Thorne, and they owned a brewery there. The major went first, then the sergeant, and they did a good job. Then, it was my turn.

Tent pegging's a rum sort of thing to do. You don't have to be daft to do it, but being a bit of a barmpot certainly helps. You have to ride down a straight track and try to pick up three little flags on the end of your lance. You have to go hell for leather, while keeping control of the horse by pressing with your knees; you can't hold the reins properly *and* hold the lance out at the same time, you see? The first two runs went better than middlin' but, on the last run, Sadie started to veer away, and I tried to lean further out, rather than correcting her with the knees and reins, like I should have. I flicked a stirrup away and stuck my heel behind the saddle, to give me more support, like. At that point I was a bit jiggered, I can tell you. Anyroad, like a silly bugger, I leaned out too far and Sadie went down. Bloody great cloud of dust, there was, and I got knocked into the middle of next week. My ribs ached like Billy-O and I couldn't breathe for ages. Then, I saw Sadie struggling to get up and I managed to stand and grab her reins. Sergeant Drew came running over to check her out and, thank the Lord, she was alright. But I wasn't. They checked me over and said I'd busted a rib or two. Trooper Stonehouse, who was the reserve, told me that Major Darley had said he had to ride in the show jumping section, instead of me. "It's a tale," I told him. He was a reight mardy bugger, was Stonehouse, and he couldn't have got a clear round in a month o' Sundays. To see him grinning at me got reight up my nose. I wasn't having none of his chelp, so I told the medical bloke to strap me up and I'd be reight as rain. There was a bit of a to-do between me and the major, and he got the monk on a bit, but he let me ride in the end, and I got a clear round on Rosie. I still ended up feeling I'd let the side down a bit though.

SESSION 2

Cavalry Training

Now, when I'd arrived at Fulford, I'd suddenly realized that it'd been one thing riding on Dora's back, as she'd dawdled her way round the cobbled streets of Hunslet, but summat quite different to stand at the side of a young, headstrong filly like Rosie, wondering how the hell I was going to get near her, never mind get on her back. You had to remember that these horses were eventually going to take you to war, and you would need them to take care of you in some pretty noisy and horrible situations. With young horses, in particular, it was very important to look after them mentally, as well as physically. Punishment is never a good way to get your pal to love you, and you really had to try to find out the cause of any bad behaviour, before trying to correct it. Just bashing away at a horse when it's playing up, only makes things worse, when it could be caused by summat as simple as a bit of badly fitted kit. When Rosie used to resist me, and after I'd checked her tackle, I must admit that I sometimes got all frustrated and bawled at her. "Now come on," I used to say, "what's the matter with you, you bloody stubborn wazzock! I've got a whip you know." But she always ignored me, and I never once hit her because I worked out that she was a high-spirited lass, with lots of power and energy to burn, and they were things that I might have to rely on in future.

At first, I was a bit scared of her, if truth be known, but I got over that when I started to realize that she needed me to take the lead and to set the boundaries. Sergeant Drew was allus there to give me tips and advice, such as how to handle plunging, which is when Rosie decided that she didn't feel comfortable doing what I was asking her to do and decided that she would toss her head, dip forrard, and then back away. He told me to grip hard with my thighs and crack the whip on my boot. That usually worked but, if it didn't, he'd tell me to pack it in and take her for a bit of a walk round, patting her and talking into her ear, and the like.

Rearing was worse, on account of it being the cause of bad injuries to the horse, the rider, and anyone standing nearby. When the horse reared you just had to go with it; there was nowt else you could do. As she was coming down you had to push forrards, so that all the energy went in that direction. Get it wrong, and up she'd go again, in any direction, which was when things could get really dodgy. It took some guts for somebody to slap her on the rear-end to make her go forrard, and a swift kick could be fatal. But, same as with most bad behaviour, rearing was caused by fear, and that was made worse by a fear of falling backards when she did it. If you did the right thing and leaned forrard, that usually stopped her panicking so much. She never *wanted* to rear, and as she was introduced to more and more of the scary things that go on in army life, it started to be pretty rare for her to do it.

We allus dismounted and led our horses towards any new experiences that were likely to fritten them, going very slowly and whispering in ears. It almost always worked, where slapping and the like, never did. If it didn't work at first, we usually tried to get them in the middle of some horses who had taken it all more calmly and walk them round again. The young horses and remounts, that had been bought by the army from farmers and the like, always seemed to benefit from that, and most of them soon got over the fear of things like saddling and getting a dose of physic, when they were done as part of a group.

I remember my first day at the riding school quite clearly; I suppose it was the biggest event in my life up to press. We'd been taught how to put on the saddle and snaffle bridles, using wooden blocks, but that first day at the school, some experienced blokes helped us put them on the real horses before we led them down to the riding school and lined up so that Sergeant Drew, who was the Riding Master, could inspect saddles, cruppers, and girths, to make sure they'd been put on properly. He ordered us to mount, which we'd also practiced on wooden dummies in the yard, but still, a few didn't manage it. The sergeant stood there all patient-like, as the ranks broke up into a bagamashings of whirling horses and bawling men. He didn't shout at all; summat I later realized was peculiar to riding instructors in the army; good ones, anyway. He told the NCOs to put cavesson padded nose bands on some of the horses and to lead the individual troopers to one side, so they could be alone with their horses. They were told to play with the nose bands and talk to the horses until they'd all calmed down, when they tried to remount. Not one of them had any trouble this time, and the NCOs just turned and led them back amongst the other horses, easy as that!

After a bit, we got some semblance of control, and the sergeant ordered us to walk round in a big circle, as he divided us into three groups. After that, he picked out some horses from each of these groups and I later learned that this was because he thought they looked a bit scared, or skittish, and needed a bit gentler handling and less energetic exercises than the others. As I say, there was no shouting, and the troopers were ordered to almost whisper words of command. I had to listen very carefully to hear the sergeant when he gave us instructions. On one occasion he told my group to dismount, and he led us all the way back to the stables, where we put our horses in their stalls. Then he took us outside and give us a reight bollocking, loud as any other sergeant in the army.

We used running reins, so we had a bit more control, but it was a big offence to tug on them and they always had to have plenty of play because

4. Cavalry Trooper in marching order. Horace Nicholls. (Wikimedia Commons)

we were told that they could make the horses move in an uncomfortable way. Anyroad, we didn't use them for long, and they did help us in the first few days.

Of course, I learned a lot about riding in those first weeks, but the most important thing was building my relationship with Rosie, and that took time. After a bit, we started learning things that were specific to cavalry riders, such as how to use bit reins so you can control a horse with one hand, while holding a sword with the other. Believe it or not, you can do this just by dividing the bit reins by the little finger of your left hand, but that's usually only the case when you're riding in a nice quiet field, with nobody else around. Try it on a battlefield and you'll usually come a cropper, pretty sharpish, at a time when your life depends on the horse turning instantly, in the reight direction. That's why, for the next couple of months, we learned how to use the horse's natural instincts to our advantage, not by trying to force them to do the unnatural, but by getting them to understand a sort of code between us, that told them what instinct to use at any specific time. That had to be simple and easily understood by the both of us, or it wouldn't work, and it took time.

I'd had basic lessons in how to hold the reins for best control, before I'd tried it out on Rosie. I'd learned that it was really important to keep her head straight when she was being asked to move in a straight line. To turn her to the right I had to hold the reins in my left hand, with the knuckles up, and pull smoothly to the right. To turn her left I had to pull to the left and bend my wrist back a bit, with the knuckles down, so my thumb pointed forrard. To pull up, I had to pull back my bent arm and straighten my back. Using the pressure of the reins against the side of the neck also tells the horse which way to turn.

It was all very simple when you did these things on a dummy horse, but quite a different matter when it came to trying them out on Rosie: as I say, she was a spirited lass. But she was also very clever, and with a bit of practice she started to get the idea, and that's when I started to feel that we were a real team.

The snaffle bit is a basic piece of kit that fits into the horse's mouth, so reins can be attached and the horse's head reasonably controlled. That's not enough though, when you're in the cavalry and you need total control in a fast-moving fight. We were taught that it was a mistake to think that some

Cavalry Training

horses had less sensitive mouths than others and so needed a tighter fitting bit and a bigger tug on the reins. Relying on sheer strength, or pain, to control a horse in battle would be impossible and wrong, as the horse would be fighting against you, rather than with you.

I started by fitting the specially measured bit into Rosie's mouth and calming her as she got used to it. Sergeant Drew told me to pat her on the neck, then move to the front and take hold of the rein near the bit ring. I had to hold up the whip so she could see it and keep mesen at arm's length as I tapped her on the chest with the whip and pointed down. She pulled backards but the sergeant told me to go with her, still tapping her chest with the whip and not saying a word. She stopped, and we tried again, with the same result, but this time when she stopped, she began to come forrards. I praised her and we did it again, making sure she saw that I was pointing down. As soon as she bent her head I poured on the praise. So simple it was, but that tiny gentle tap and pointing of the whip was now like a whole conversation between us whenever I needed her to come forward and follow the direction of the whip. After that, I was taught how to get her comfortable with the bit, by playing with it while I was stood by her. I found that pulling gently on one side led to her moving her head that way, and we did this for ages before trying it from the saddle. Straight away, she started to pull her head from side to side and Sergeant Drew told me to stop twitching. He pointed to my hands, and I realized just how much I was fiddling with the reins without thinking about it. As her head moved from side to side, I was trying to control it by pulling and tugging, which made her even worse. I think I might have fallen off if I hadn't heard the sergeant and realized what he was on about. The whole idea was to get Rosie to move her head when I gave her the signal with the lightest of touches. As I say, she was always going to move in the direction her head was pointing, so I had to be very, very careful with all my hand movements. After a while, if I kept making sure that any head movement I didn't want was corrected by a gentle pressure from the bit, she wouldn't take badly to my instructions. Bad riding leads to a horse that can't respond to the bit, and in the case of a cavalry horse, that can be fatal when you need full control in a melee, or single combat.

We got taught how to control the horse using the knees, how to circle to the right and to the left, on the forehand and the haunches, trotting, bending, reining back, and cantering, as individuals and in groups. Over many weeks we practiced and practiced these skills. We got accustomed to the orders and used to carry them out sharpish: "change leg," "half passage," "move off by your right at a walk," "close your files," "trot," and everything at a faster and faster pace. "Rein back," "use the spur," "go about on the forehand," and "go about on the haunches," were carried out by instinct. I was looked on as a "leading file" because I could do these things quicker than most, and with the horse moving at a faster pace. Still, Sergeant Drew was forever chelping on to me about the position of my hands and body. I can still hear his quiet but clear voice: "elbows back, hands low, head up, heels low!"

During all of this we were introduced to using a sword, both mounted and dismounted, and it was then that all the practice at controlling a horse with just the use of knees and one hand, started to make real sense. We also had musketry practice, as they wanted us to be as good at shooting as the infantry.

We had Lee-Enfield rifles that were shorter than normal rifles and they were bolt-action repeaters that could fire from a 5-round charger, or "clip."

We got the horses used to the feel of fighting, by wrapping swords in cloth to stop them rattling, and by waving them about, gently at first, then more aggressively, accompanied by shouting. They got used to things by degrees, spread over the whole period of the training, and we rode them

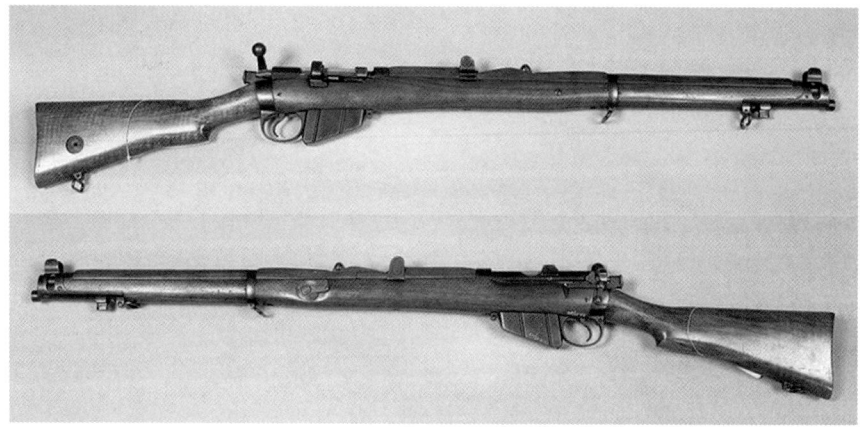

5. Lee-Enfield SMLE Mk III (No 1 Mk 3) Calibre .303. The Swedish Army Museum. (Wikimedia Commons)

through fireworks, drums, and flares. When we fired from horseback, we turned the horses towards the target and stretched out an arm so we could rest the rifle on it. We leaned forrard and made sure the muzzle was well out in front of the horse's face when we fired. I found that being relaxed helped Rosie to relax too. We tied the reins to a stake in the ground when we were ordered to dismount and fire, but after some practice, we found that we didn't need to, as the horses just waited for us.

We were ready for action, I suppose.

SESSION 3

Afridi Campaign

Now, I know I'm a bit of a nesh 'un, but it was clap cold in France, that winter of 39–40. They say it was the coldest on record and we had to load the horses onto another train because we were going south. The water troughs were frozen, and we had to break the ice so we could fill our buckets. Funny, I'd always reckoned France was a warm sort of place, but not that year. We had the Yorkshire Hussars and the Sherwood Rangers for company, and they called us the 5th Cavalry Brigade of the 1st Cavalry Division. We'd met them before we'd sailed to Dieppe, and now they were loading up with us, on the way to Marseilles. You see, we weren't going to fight Germans, we were going to Palestine, and although that was a bit of a bugger, at least it would be hot. I was used to hot places, what with having been in India just a few years earlier.

That had been after joining the Hussars in 1927, and after there'd been a bit of a palaver on account of me having been wagging it in Leeds. I'd met a lass called Violet, who was a bit of a warm 'un, and I sort of fell for her and I stayed a bit too long, even though they'd already given me a Scarborough warning before I'd left. They had me up for being absent without leave, and after a 28-day stint in Aldershot glasshouse, I got transferred to the 15/19th Hussars, because the 14/20th had already left for India. I wasn't reight chuffed by that, on account of how I'd enjoyed my time in the 14/20th and I was going to miss my best mukka, Ben. He could chelp like nobody's business, and he was daft as a brush, but real mukkas are hard to come by, aren't they?

Even though they'd told me she was a bit of a puddin' burner, I still carried a torch for Violet, until I got back from India, and she'd buggered off after another bloke. I'd had her name tattooed on my arm anall. That was summat that didn't go down well with your mum when I met her. She allus used to wind me up about it whenever she could. Still does.

As I say, we'd had some fun had me and Ben, especially when we got dressed up as Russians during the filming of the film "Balaclava" that starred Cyril McLaglen and Benita Hulme. They were big stars back then, you know. It was one of the perks of being in the cavalry, getting jobs like that. We got to wear long, grey coits, black fur hats, and big, baggy breeches, and we charged at another lot of cavalry, who were dressed up as French Chasseurs from the Crimean War. I managed to half-inch a nice set of stirrups and a horse's bit, but I lost them later, as usual. Some folks are just careless when they're youngsters, aren't they? Two other blokes weren't as lucky and got killed when a cannon blew up while they were packing a blank charge. Anyway, all that malarky was over now. I was off to Egypt with my new regiment.

We sailed from Southampton to Alexandria, and I remember, just as if it were yesterday, watching the Isle of Wight disappear over the horizon. That made me feel a bit homesick, soft apeth that I was. I soon got over that on account of being bloody seasick for almost all of the voyage. By 'eck I felt rough! Then they told us we were moving straight on to Bombay. Bombay! I bloody ask you!

6. Cavalry charge from "Balaclava". Filmed at Aldershot Arena (UK). Release date: 6 June 1928 (UK). Directors: Elvey. M/Rosmer. M. Production Company: Gainsborough Pictures. (YouTube)

I was chucking up all the way to the Suez Canal but then it calmed down and we went through the Red Sea, the Gulf of Aden and then the Arabian Sea. I liked to watch the dolphins racing in our bow wave, and I waved to the Arabs in the dhows that we passed. Sharks were allus following us, trying to pick up the rubbish that got tipped overboard. Some of the lads used them for target practice, but I didn't on account of I reckoned it was cruel. I never said owt to them though. You just didn't do that if you wanted to stay pally, you know.

Bombay was a shock to the system, even though I only saw it from the train as it trundled along. It was my first look at India, and I was fair gobsmacked by all the noise and colours and smells. It was boiling hot, and I'd been lathered, even before we got off the ship. Then, they stuck us in this train where we had to sit shoulder to shoulder, while twenty Indians climbed up on the roof. For a change, the horses had their own trucks. They were happy as Larry.

As usual, we had no idea where we were going, except that it was north. It cooled down a bit when we got moving and a breeze started blowing through the windows. We went across some wide plains that were that big you couldn't see an end to them. Sometimes, we saw a few village huts, mutti huts they called them. They were made of cow pats and straw, or so I found out when I was earwigging a conversation between two of the Sherwoods and one of them said he'd been out there before. Must've stunk to high-heaven, I thought. Bairns used to run alongside us so we could throw our chocolate rations to them. Beautiful, happy bairns, they were. I even saw a tiger reight up near the track. I think it must've come out of the forest to have a look-see what all the commotion was about. Anyroad, it wasn't a bad journey, I suppose. We got to the foothills of some mountains and ended up at a place called Risalpur. Spring of 1930, that was.

Risalpur was a cantonment, about 40 miles from the Khyber Pass, and we were stationed there to try to protect the north of India from the Afghan tribesmen. They were raiding Indian villages all the time, and we had to try to stop them. The main cantonment was about a mile from the railway station, and they reckoned it was secure, but they reckoned without the locals, who used to sneak in and half-inch stuff from our barracks. Some of the lads got left with Sweet Fanny Adams. They doubled the guard, but the buggers still got in. They pinched the last letter I'd had from my mum before Dad wrote and told me she'd died of septicaemia, after a miscarriage.

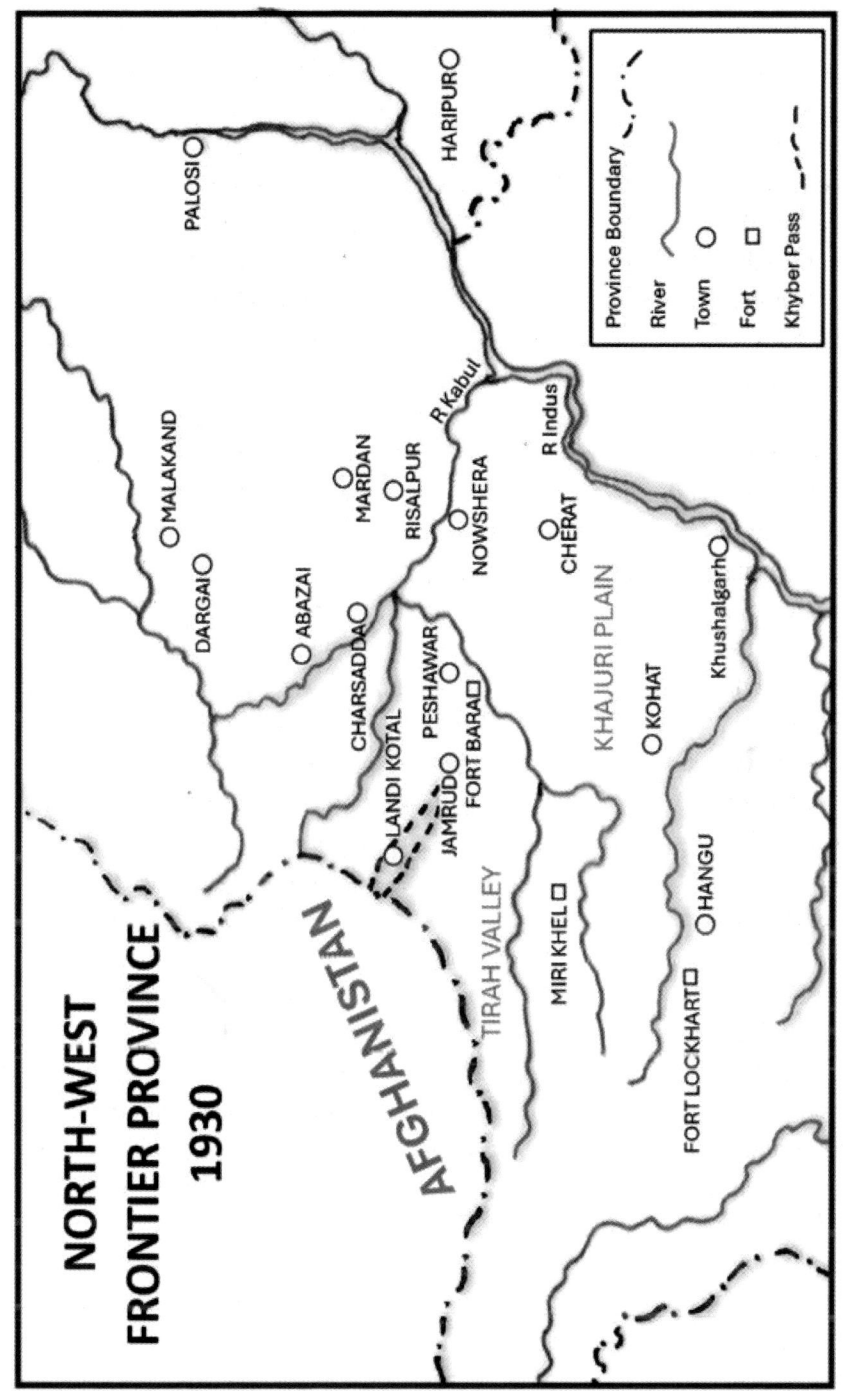

The Afridis were the main offenders when it came to the raids on the villages. They were supposed to be causing trouble as part of the Indian independence movement who all wore red shirts as a sort of uniform, but they didn't half do some looting and killing in the process, and I saw some reight sights. We didn't have much love for the Afridis, I can tell you.

Mind you, they didn't love us too much either and it all got stirred up when a protest in Peshawar got out of hand. It seems that the Indian Police couldn't cope, and the army went in, all heavy-handed like, and opened fire on the redshirts and some innocent civilians. A lot of people died and the Afridis doubled up their attacks after that.

In the summer, we got sent out into the Khajuri Plain, which is west of Peshawar and south of the Khyber Pass, where we were supposed to protect the infantry as they made roads across the valley. One day we got sent to check up on two forts, I can't remember their names. Anyroad, they were quite close to each other, and we were told there were hundreds of Afridis holed up there.

7. British Indian Army soldiers in Peshawar, 1930. Unknown. (Wikimedia Commons)

We ended up in a shallow ravine, a nullah they called it, and it was reight between these two forts, that were only about half a mile apart. The nullah wasn't that deep, but we could leave the horses in it, out of the sun, and crawl up to the top of it to have a look what was going on. I was in the machine gun troop, with Trooper Ellis and Trooper Cunningham. Ellis was number one and carried the gun tripod. I was number two and got the Vickers 303, for my sins, and Cunningham dragged up the ammunition box and cooling tank for the gun. When we reached the top, Ellis was supposed to kneel and set up the tripod by holding onto its back leg and tossing out the other two, but he knelt up too high and a dum-dum bullet hit him in the chest. Poor sod lay there screaming and I shouted out for help. First time I'd ever seen someone shot, that was, and I chucked up.

I couldn't hang about though. We were under fire from one of the forts and I had to get the tripod set up while Cunningham attached the ammunition and water tank. I fired the Vickers at what looked like a tower at the edge of one of the forts. Well, I can tell you, those bullets made a reight mess of it. I think it must have been made of mud, or some such, like the muttis, because the 303s ripped it to shreds, and bits and pieces were flying all over the place. There was this great cloud of dust, and we were coughing and spluttering like good 'uns, but the Afridis weren't giving up. Oh no! Not by a long chalk. They took ages to give up the ghost, and I thought they were going to keep on firing 'til the cows came home! We didn't half give 'em what for, but they were still a bugger to shift.

When they did come out, they were waving a bit of rag tied to a stick, but it wasn't the Afridis, it was a gaggle of lasses and bairns. They were dressed up in long brown robes that covered them from head to foot, and they walked slowly across the nullah and into the second fort. We reckoned they were getting out of the firing line before the men came out.

Well, I'd allus thought you'd got to be up early to pull the wool over *my* eyes, but bugger me, if the sods we'd just watched didn't start firing at us from behind. In fairness, I think everybody thought they were lasses and bairns, but we'd been played like a fiddle. Some of our lads crawled across to give us cover from another direction and we kept firing, in spurts, all afternoon.

As soon as it got dark, they told us to pack up and move out, and we managed it without any more shooting. I suppose they were as fed up as

8. A group of Afridi warriors at the Jamrud Fort. Shepherd. C. (Wikimedia Commons)

we were. They hadn't killed any of our horses, so we mounted up and rode the fifty miles back to Risalpur. They told us later that the Afridis had buggered off home too, and we hoped we'd seen the back of them, but no such luck. They kept going back to the Khyber Pass, where they could hide out in the mountain foothills, then keep coming out to have a go at the building sites where the army was building strongpoints.

In the autumn of 1930, things had got so bad that we went out into the Tirah Valley, about 50 miles outside Peshawar, and started doing patrols while a strongpoint was built at Miri Khel. That was supposed to be a base that could be used to react to Afridi sightings more quickly, so when we were called out to another village, we got there in time to join up with some infantry from the Green Howards, even though they'd come from Nowshera, which was a lot closer to the village than we were. Anyroad, we were expecting big trouble as we got there, but in fact, we sorted things without much fuss or drama. The Green Howards marched the Afridi men into the main square and made them sit down, with their hands on their heads. They were impressive blokes, the Afridis. It was the first time I'd seen any of them up close and we'd always thought of them like you think of boggarts, that appeared and disappeared in the night and left you all jittery and flummoxed. They all seemed to be over six foot tall, but I suppose some of that was to do with the pugaris that they wound around their heads. Golden brown colour, they were, all golden brown in these baggy gowns and pugaris, and they looked down at us as if we were summat they'd wiped off their shoes. They just weren't used to gettin' beat, I suppose. In the end, we were pulled out in January of 1931 because the raids stopped, and we all got the North-West Frontier medal.

SESSION 4

Sheep's Eyeballs and a Scuttled Ship

We were in a reight state by the time we landed at Haifa in early March 1940, I reckon it must've been. Lieutenant-Colonel Stephenson was in command of the regiment because Colonel Warde-Aldam was ill, and we'd had to leave him behind.

At Marseilles, we'd been camped in the grounds of the Château de la Reynarde, which was perched on a hill above us. The weather was still horrible, and everything was covered in deep snow. We tried to pitch our tents in the lee of a drystone wall that ran around the grounds, but everybody was fighting for a place there, so some had to grin and bear it, out in the wind. I got a bit jammy and managed to smarm my way into a tent near the wall. By 'eck, it was clap cold and biting, that wind, I'm telling you, and it was the horses that got the worst of it. We tried to make them as comfortable as we could, and I made sure that Flash had three thicknesses of blankets over him, but one poor bugger wasn't that lucky. I don't suppose the trooper had thought about what might happen to the horse at the end of the line, when he'd tied her up there, but I could see something was wrong, as soon as I went on piquet duty.

For a start, she was a brown mare, but that night, she was white on one side. The freezing wind had hit her full on, and icicles hung from the white side of her blanket. I walked round to the brown side, and she didn't move at all, so I reached out and patted her rump. Well, down she went like she was made of stone; she just toppled over on stiff legs, into a drift of snow. I know it sounds daft, but the thought came to me that if I'd patted her other rump, she might have brought the whole line down, like dominoes. I shouted to my mukka on piquet duty to fetch a vet, while I ran to check on Flash, who was fine and just looked at me like I was addled. I gave him a hug.

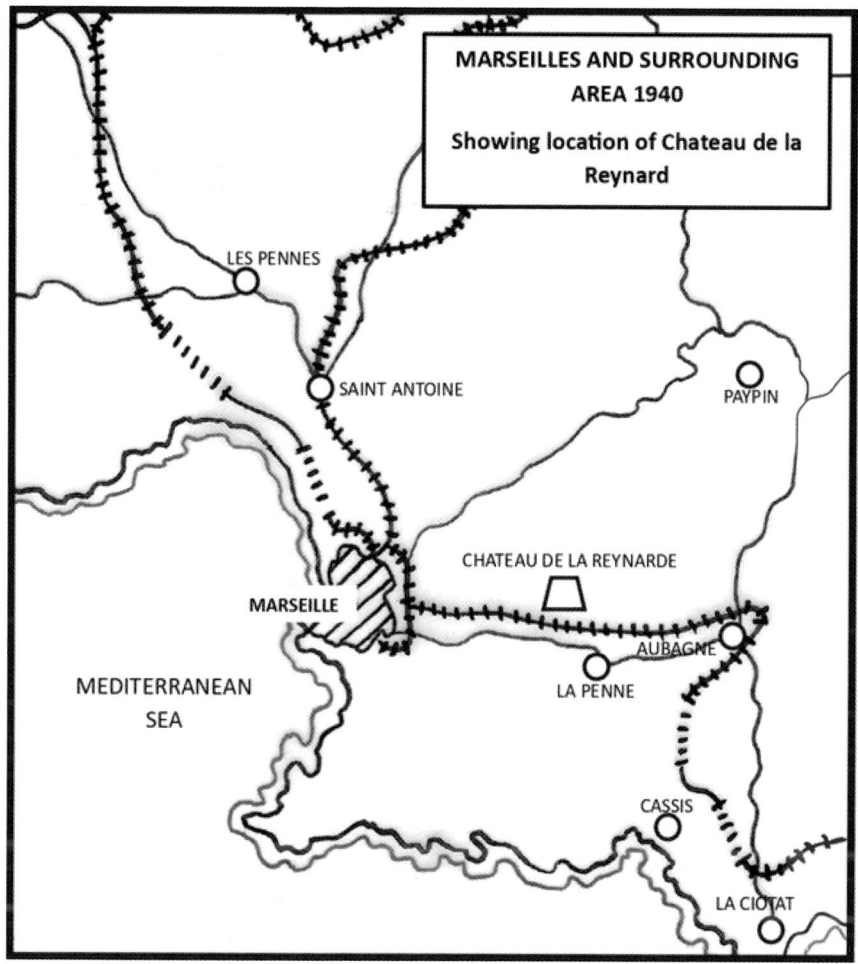

The blizzard continued for several days, and we built a snow wall around the horses, to protect them from the wind. The supply lorries managed to climb up to us along icy roads that were a bugger to keep clear, and we spread bales of hay in the snow paddocks and tried to tie tarpaulin sheets over them. It wasn't much, but we piled all the blankets we had spare, onto the horse's backs, and set up a rota of checks on them, making sure that the temporary troughs were always clear of ice. A veterinary officer got frostbite and was ferried out to a sick bay in one of the ships that were starting to arrive in Marseilles to shift us all out of France. I heard he had some fingers amputated.

One day, the wind and snow stopped long enough for me and "Bog-arse" Wilson to suggest that we might go down to the harbour to see if we could get any gen on when we might be moving. We added that we might be able to half-inch some booze and fags from stores, and the captain gave us permission to go, even though he said he'd deny all knowledge of thieving, if we were caught. That was enough for us.

We cadged a lift on one of the returning supply lorries, and after passing by a beautiful church on the hill, we were dropped off in what we were told was the "Old Port". The quayside was packed with people all going about their business, and the water was full of fishing boats. Further out, we could see a big transport ship, and we wondered if it would be the one waiting to pick us up. Bog-arse grabbed hold of my arm and pointed towards a café-bar that seemed very dodgy-looking to me. Against my better judgement I allowed him to drag me out of the evening sunlight and into the dingy pub.

A little girl of about six or seven, held out her hand to me, and without thinking, I took it. She'd led me a few steps towards the bar, when a woman, who I thought might be her mother, grabbed hold of her and jerked her away from me. She was a rather old-looking woman, with prominent cheek bones and a nose like a beak. She slapped the girl a fair wallop that sent the little mite flying through the gap between two barrels that supported the top of the bar. I stepped forrard and was just going to give the old woman a gob full when I felt summat pressing into my back. A bloke mumbled summat in French. I can't speak the language, but the voice spoke all calm-like, so I turned round and fair messed mesen when I saw a bloody great shotgun pointed at my nose.

The man grinned at me. I remember he had a golden front tooth that made him look like a bloody pirate. He rubbed his trigger finger against his thumb and said summat like "frick?" I was too bothered about the way his finger was moving about, so close to the flaming trigger, to say owt, so I just grinned back.

The woman looked at me and said, "money." I wanted to think she was being helpful, but her look made me doubt it.

She shouted again. "Money!" and this time I got the message.

I din't see that I had any choice, so I pulled out the bag holding the booze kitty, real slow like.

The man's eyes went that wide I thought they'd jump out of his head, but he just chucked the gun behind the bar and clapped me round the shoulders, like we were old mukkas. He jerked a hand in the general direction of the old bint that I thought must be his wife, and she fiddled about under the bar a bit, before bringing out three glasses and a bottle of green stuff.

"Absinthe?" the old bugger said. He had a smile that false it made me shudder. Horrible it was. Like a bloody dog just before it tries to bite yer leg off.

I was pretty well set against drinking owt green, but Bog-arse was well known for supping owt that was free. We even got him to sup meths, one time. He said it wasn't bad. Anyway, he hardly looked at the glass that got handed to him, before swilling it down his neck. He said nowt; just held out the glass for a refill.

I sniffed at my drink before I sipped it. It tasted a bit like the aniseed balls we used to suck on when we were kids. It really wasn't that bad. I chucked it back.

Later, I found out that the stuff was called Arak, by the Arabs, and a few glasses of it used to line your stomach so that you could get drunk for the next couple of days, just by drinking water. I only did it the once; that was enough for me.

Bog-arse was reaching for the bottle again when the barman held out his hand and rubbed his fingers together again. I got the message and held out a handful of cash for him to take what he wanted. What he wanted was a hell of a bloody lot!

I told him it was too much, and I must've looked like I meant it because he shrugged and put the bottle away. I handed over a few notes and he seemed satisfied, so that told me he would've robbed us blind if I'd let him.

Bog-arse asked if there was any beer, and they seemed to understand that. In a couple of shakes of a rats tail, two opened bottles slid down the bar in our direction. The beer was a bit warm, but it was still pretty good.

"How much?" I said.

The sneaky bugger pulled a note from the stack in my hand and I held up my fingers to show him how many bottles I wanted. I figured we could afford twenty, and that would amount to about two crateful's. Me and Bog-arse would sup the rest of the cash away. The man seemed to get the message and disappeared out the back.

Looking round the room for the first time, I took in the unfriendly faces that stared at me. The woman with the beak for a nose was dipping almonds into a saucer of summat, and she eyed me like I was lousey, as she shoved a nut into her gob and bit down on it that hard, it made me shiver. I wouldn't want to meet her in a dark alley at night!

The barman came back, holding a crate of beer, and I held up two fingers. He tried to look puzzled, but his acting was rubbish. He was trying to work a fast one on us again and I was having none of it. I held up the wad of notes and waved it under his nose, and he went out to fetch another crate. When he came back, he slammed the second crate down on the bar. He tried to grab the cash out of my hand, but I pulled it back, quick as a flash.

"Not until we walk out the door," I said, and I pointed to the entrance. He seemed to understand that, and I got the impression that he knew more English than he was letting on.

Bog-arse had moved over to where the old woman was sitting, and he was dipping a finger into the saucer in front of her. She slapped his hand away, but he still managed to scoop up some of the stuff. He stuck it in his gob. He really was disgusting, was old Bog-arse.

"Bloody garlic!" he shouted, and the woman slapped him as if he'd done summat horrible to her. I don't know whether it was the slap that made him pull a face, or the fact that he didn't like garlic. Never asked him.

A couple of hours later, we were all pretty addled. I'd worked out the price of the two crates, and I'd done the sums to work out how much that was for a bottle. Then, we'd just stayed put, using up the banknotes as we knocked back the beer.

The absinthe was obviously far too pricey, and we'd turned to calvados, as a change from beer. It was only a little bit more expensive. Bog-arse and his new lady friend had started drinking an evil-looking mix of absinthe and calvados, as they noshed their way through a pile of almonds and made eyes at each other. Even though I was pretty sozzled I was still sober enough to realize that we'd almost used up the wad of notes in my pocket and that we hadn't actually paid for the crates of ale that were still stood standing on the bar.

I surmised that Bog-arse was too half-cut to get that the money was almost gone, and we were in big trouble because we hadn't enough to pay for the crates the lads in camp were expecting. They'd flay us alive if we went back empty handed and without their cash. Still, I whispered in his ear and hoped for the best. He gave me a drunken wink and nodded at the two crates. Then, he winked again.

"When I give the signal," he said, slurring his words so that even I struggled to understand them. Nobody else seemed to have a clue.

I gave Bog-arse a hard stare, as I handed over the last of the cash to the bar owner, and at that moment he let out one of the enormous farts that had made him a legend in the squadron. When his lady friend fell off her stool, he let out another ripsnorter, and everyone else covered their mouths in disgust. A third fart nearly took the roof off, and as the barman dived into the back room, Bog-arse shot up, grabbed one of the crates of beer, and flew out the door. Well, I didn't need a lot of prompting. I picked up the other crate and charged out into the street as if the Devil himself was after me, which indeed he was. Well, not exactly Lucifer, but Lucien the barman was close enough. As we belted down the dockside, knocking people out of the way, he tried to run and load the shotgun at the same time. Luckily for us, he kept dropping the cartridges, and we had found an army lorry just as he at last managed to get the thing loaded. The lorry driver took in the scene at a glance, and in an icy skid, turned to expose the open tail gate for us to dive aboard. The gun blasted out and the tarpaulin around us was ripped by shot, and I turned to see the old man standing there, shaking the shotgun in the air, and shouting "you filthy bastards!"

As we sped out of Old Port, I remember thinking that his English wasn't too bad after all.

We were pleased as punch to be marching down to Marseilles docks next day, I can tell you, even though it was hard to look at the French folk who peeked at us from behind curtains. We were deserting them, and they knew it. The cobbles were frozen, and we went slipping and sliding all the way to the gangplanks of an Australian auxiliary ship that was waiting for us. She'd had an extra deck added, so she could take more troops, but that made her top-heavy, and we were going to know all about what that meant. We put the horses into the stalls that ran down each side of the lower deck, and we were billeted on the top deck. Well, we managed alright until we sailed out of Marseilles harbour and into a bloody great storm. You imagine mucking out a set of jam-packed stalls, in a ship that's rolling and tossing around like Billy-O! To start with, we had to move the first horse in the line

9. HMAS Vampire and HMAS Voyager encrusted with ice. Marseilles Harbour 1940. McDonald D J. (www.awm.gov.au)

out of its stall and lead it into a small gap at one end if the deck. We had to clean its stall out and then move the horse that was in the next stall, into the clean stall. Do you get me? Then, we had to do the same thing all down the line and, finally, put the first horse in the last stall. It was smelly, hard work, it went on for hours, and all the while most of us were puking-up like good 'uns.

As I said, that extra deck made the ship roll and pitch all over the place, even in a calm sea, but we went through a storm all the way from Marseilles to Greece and, yet again, the horses suffered summat rotten. I think seven or eight died during the voyage and they had to slit open their bellies so they would sink when they were tipped over the side; we didn't want any U-boats picking up our trail, you see.

When we landed at Haifa, we had to have all the horses checked out by vets, and it took a long time to get them fit again. Eventually though, we moved out along the coast road, towards Mount Carmel. Bairns were playing in the street as we rode by, and they cadged sweets off us, as usual.

Then, we camped on the edge of the Plains of Esdraelon, underneath a monastery that was perched on a hill. They told us that the Plains of Esdraelon were where the Battle of Armageddon was going to happen, at the end of the world, like. I thought I'd already witnessed summat of the kind, at Hunslet Irish Centre, on Saint Paddy's night, 1926. By 'eck, that potcheen's powerful stuff!

Major Simpson made a point of going round to each tent to tell us to make sure that we put our bed boards on posts. He said they were to be at least three feet high because of scorpions. I thought he was just being a bit of a wazzock, trying to fritten us all, but next day, as I got dressed, I shoved my hand into my boot and got stung by one of the buggers. By 'eck it hurt like blazes! I ran to the medical tent and joined the queue. They sorted me out. It could've been worse: one lad got stung on the backside, and that's not good news for a horse soldier. It was weeks before the poor bugger could ride again.

After my arm had gone down a bit, I started to take Flash out for a ride every day. My usual route was across the plains, through the Mus-Mus pass and on towards Khirbat: about twenty miles all told. We used to go to Kiryat beach for a swim, and that was a bit of a resort where the locals came on outings. They all seemed to speak English, and many a time I got invited into some tea rooms, for a brew and a chinwag.

Sometimes I had to eat sheep's eyeballs and burp, but that was only when I had to go on courtesy calls, to the Arab villages, in the company of a major who spoke Arabic. Can't remember his name. We were trying to keep the Arabs on our side, you see, so we had to go round and try to butter them up. We used to sit, crossed legged, in the Muktah's gudoun, that means the chief's tent, and drink coffee that strong you could stand the spoon up in it. All black and sweet and it clagged-up yer clacker, but it was alreight when you got used to it. They gave us all sorts of grub and most of it weren't too bad, but the sheep's eyeballs used to pop in your mouth, like a balloon filled with jelly. Urgh! They stared back at you as you ate them, and you had to burp, or else that meant you hadn't enjoyed them. The Arabs were sticklers for good manners and got the monk on dead easy, if they thought you'd insulted them. We allus took some food with us, from army rations, and the bairns loved it. They allus crowded round us when we got there.

10. Sergeant Harry Holgate, the Plains of Esdraelon, Palestine 1940. (Roger Holgate)

We'd ask the Muktah and his lads about where they'd seen the Italians, and such things. We learned a lot about the desert from them blokes, and we made a lot of friends: something that was going to come in very handy in the near future, when we would need all the friends we could get.

The Jews and the Arabs were allus at each other's throats and that caused trouble for us too. It was only minor trouble because Palestine's a big place and they usually managed to stay apart, but one morning I started to have an inkling that this state-of-affairs wasn't going to last.

We were ordered up to Kiryat beach in Haifa Bay, and as usual, we were looking forrard to letting the horses have a run in the sea. As soon as we got there, though, we could see that a big freighter was anchored offshore, and boatloads of people were being rowed towards us. This wasn't going to be a day off, not by a long chalk.

11. After a tribal lunch at cavalry post at Tel-el-Meleiha, 20 miles North of Beersheba, 18th January 1940. G. Eric and Edith Matson. (Wikimedia Commons)

We sat there watching, as the first boat reached the beach and its load of people jumped in and ran ashore. They dropped to their knees, every one of them, and kissed the sand. Some of them lifted their hands up to the sky and it was obvious who they were. We'd got wind that the Jews were being badly treated in Germany, but not the stuff that came out later. Your mum's boss, old Sammy Morris, had Jewish relatives in Austria and he told her some reight tales about how they were being treated, and how they were trying to get to Palestine. We didn't know owt about mass-murders and the like, back then. We only found out that stuff years later. Anyroad, these folk looked very European in how they were dressed: not reight for the African desert, that's for sure.

The major told us to round them up, and we did as we were told, as usual. We tear-arsed down from the dunes and tried to make a circle around them, but there were some on the edge of the group that started to run. There wasn't much time to think about it, and we wouldn't have known what to think even if there had been, so a few of us chased after

12. View of Haifa Bay from Mount Carmel c. 1911. Kiryat Beach is on the right. Unknown. (Wikimedia Commons)

the runners. I started after this young lad, who was probably in his late teens, from what I remember, and he started scrambling up a sand dune. I got him of course; Flash caught up with him in a few strides, but he tried to keep running and I grabbed hold of his collar and hauled him off the ground. The poor sod kept struggling, so I had to jump off and get a proper hold of him. His eyes were nearly bulging out of his head, poor little bugger, and I remember feeling ashamed, though I wasn't sure why. I think I said summat like "come on sunshine" or summat like that, and I took hold of Flash's reins in one hand, and the lad's collar in the other, and walked them back to the major.

The refugees were all huddled together, in their heavy coits and Sunday-best titfers. We were all looking sheepishly at the major, who glared back at us, as if he was trying to say it wasn't his fault. Anyroad, he told us to put them back in the boats, so they could be rowed back to the ship. There was some chelping from our lads, and he had to tell us that we couldn't let them go because the Arabs would knock seven bells out of them if we did. That's how it was, back then. So, we started shepherding them back to the boats, still chuntering as we went. They were all crying and wailing and the like. It was a bad job all round.

Then we heard the freighter sound its hooter and everybody looked up to see what the commotion was all about. Slowly, it dawned on us that the ship was sinking, and later on, when I went earwigging at the major's tent, I found out that the crew had scuttled it when they saw what we were up to. So, we lifted them out of the boats again, and we all settled down to wait for orders about what we were going to do next. We sat around all day, faffing about with the horses and sharing our ration packs with the Jews, and such like, but generally not talking to them too much: I suppose we didn't want to get involved any more than we had to, because we all felt like bad buggers.

Then, the engineers turned up and started building a compound out of poles and wire netting, and we guarded that compound, on and off, for two months. Every so often, we saw little groups being released from the compound, and they told us that they were all going off to kibbutzes, which were these little Jewish settlements out in the desert, where they all lived sort of communal-like, and on account of how I'd allus been a bit of a socialist, the idea sounded good to me. We let them go in family groups, a bit at a time, so the Arabs wouldn't notice.

Not long after, I got ordered to go on a gunnery instructor's course at Sarafand: that's about 40 miles north of Haifa. I rode there on my own, and set off one afternoon, meaning to sleep at the roadside, in my sleeping bag, but as it turned out, I came across a kibbutz, just as it started to get dark. Near Tyre, I think it was. Anyroad, I tell you, they didn't half take care of us. They took Flash to the stable, and me for some supper. It was good stuff anall: fresh-baked bread and some sort of soup with dumplings floating in it. I had red wine and peaches, summat I'd never had before, then I had a shower and they let me sleep in a comfy bed. That was better than sleeping in the desert, by a long chalk.

Next morning, I had breakfast, gave the bairns my chocolate ration, and waved back as they waved me off. I'll never forget those people and it got me thinking that living in a community, where everybody was treated equal, wasn't such a bad idea.

When I got to Sarafand I saw a big internment camp where they were putting illegal immigrants, and I remember thinking, "what a bloody world!"

> 547113 Sgt. Holgate
> "B" Squadron
> QOYD
> Middle East Forces
> Sunday 15-12-40

Dear Kitty and Alf

Many thanks for your most welcome letter which I received about a week ago but have been unable to answer owing to the fact that I have been very busy indeed. I know you will understand. Well Kitty, I am so glad to hear that you are all in the very best of health, and also that the bombers are leaving our district alone. So glad to know that Mary and the kiddies are alright, I know when you say so that it is right. Of course, Mary tells me in every letter that they are well, but I know Mary, she would tell me that because she wouldn't want to upset me.

You say that the garden is yielding a good crop of marrows and other vegetables; well, that's more than I would be able to get out of it, but then I wasn't much of a gardener. Remember, in your letter you asked me if there was anything that I would have liked to have got for the kiddies for Xmas, if so to let you know. Well Kitty, I couldn't think of a thing and even if I could it would have been too late before you got to know from me. Anyway, many thanks for your very kind thoughts. Just a little note to Mum. I think she will think I have forgotten her:

Hello Love! How are you keeping in this big upset? In good health and spirits, I hope.

Well Mum, after this is all over, you will be able to walk about again knowing that you can go to sleep at night without being disturbed. That's what makes us determined to win through, to clear the air of all bad feeling, so that the next generation will be left in peace and security. You will know now, as I write this, that our time has come and the boys are doing their fair share out here, and the way things are going, it won't last long.

Well, this is all I have time to write just now, so au revoir till we meet again with oceans of love and kisses.

From your ever-loving son, Harry. xxxxxxxx
Goodnight and God bless you all at home. xxxxxxxxxxx
Julie xx Pat xx Carroll xx
Pint of Warwick's for Alf.

SESSION 5

Ghandi, an Air Crash, and the Punkah Wallah

I'll not forget the Indians either. They were a rum lot back in 1932 and were getting all stirred up by Ghandi. You've heard of him: he was the bloke that got independence for India, in the end. We got copies of old newspapers from England at that time, and I saw some articles about how he'd been to some cotton mills in Lancashire, and how the workers had taken to him and

13. Ghandi at a protest meeting, Peshawar, North-West Frontier. Unknown. (Wikimedia Commons)

cheered him on when he'd told them how the Indian cotton workers were getting treated. Now, I'd been inside a cotton mill, in Yorkshire, and if the conditions in India were worse than what I'd seen there, they must've been pretty grim. Anyroad, the British workers supported the Indian workers and that's how it *should* be, I reckon.

Still, us soldiers had a different view of Ghandi, because of what we'd seen. You see, he allus called for peaceful protest but we saw summat else altogether. Those who followed him used to wear red shirts and most of them were just a pain in the backside: chuntering and being mardy and blocking roads, and the like. Some of them though, started carting guns around. They used to hang them from Sam Brownes and swan around like Soft Mick, but sometimes they would start firing and that's when we had to step in.

When we got ordered to a village one day, for the umpteenth time, to sort out some looting and the like, we weren't exactly pleased as punch. We could hear the racket as we crossed the local miadan, and then the Indian Police told us it was all kicking off. They asked us to surround the place while they went in and sorted out the troublemakers, so that's what we did. We moved in, like a noose, as the police started braying the blokes in red shirts, which was a bad job as far as I was concerned. There were shots, and the braying got worse until it looked like a bloody big riot was going on. All we could do was spur the horses and close the ring, so the police could take control. They hated us, them redshirts, and we weren't too unhappy to see them loaded into lorries and carted off to Rawalpindi gaol, while we went back to Risalpur.

I liked Risalpur and we had some good times there; I even learned to speak Hindustani. Then, something happened that shook me up summat rotten, and that's no lie. One day, I was sitting on the veranda of the sergeant's mess, (beautiful spot that was) looking out over the mountains and smelling the jasmine and rajanigandha, when I spotted a cloud of dust that was moving across the plain, right towards me. It turned out to be a cartload of RAF trucks and they came driving into the parade square in front of me, before blokes started chucking out all sorts of gear. The first aircraft arrived a few hours later, and then they all started coming, until there was about a dozen, in all. The pilots were billeted near us, so we got to know them quite well, in no time.

A couple of weeks later, we were all having a beer and a bit of snap in the sergeant's mess, when I got talking to one of the pilots, I can't remember his name for the life of me, and he told me all about his machine. I wasn't bored or owt, like some people were, and me and Charlie Harris sat there for ages, listening. The pilot had a Hawker Hart bi-plane and that was a two-seater bomber. It was the latest thing, and he was proper proud of it. A long time afterward, I found out it'd been designed by the same feller who designed the Spitfire, you know. It was a real bobby-dazzler, anyroad, and the pilot was so proud of it that he and his mate offered to take me and Charlie Harris for a fly around.

I was a bit unnerved, to tell the truth, but I wasn't going to say so, and before you could say Jack Robinson, there I was, sitting behind the pilot, leather helmet on my head, and tear-arsing down the runway, towards the Himalayas.

When I opened my eyes, we were banking over our cantonment and soaring like one of the eagles we used to see all the time. Well, I just sat there gawping until the other Hart came alongside and we both shot off in the general direction of the Khyber Pass. My pilot went down low and skimmed the Indian border post and barracks. Somebody waved as we flew over, and then I could see the Afghan border, which was hard to miss because somebody had painted a bloody great big, thick white line on the road.

14. Hawker Hart. Unknown. (Wikipedia)

Ghandi, an Air Crash, and the Punkah Wallah

We flew a bit further and I got a bit panicky again because we weren't supposed to be there, in Afghanistan like, and sure enough, before long, there was a puff of white smoke below us and Charlie's Hart seemed to buck, like a horse does when you saddle it for the first time. The pilot slumped forrard, and for a couple of seconds, the nose dropped. Then, he seemed to get it back under control, but how the hell an Afghan had managed to hit an aircraft, with a musket ball, I hadn't a clue. Still haven't. Say what you like, they were top shots, the Afghans.

We followed the Hart all the way back to Risalpur, feeling about as much use as a chocolate fireguard, and it seemed that they were going to make it, even though the Hart was wobbling a bit. Then the wheels touched the ground, and the thing went arse-over-tit and hit the ground again like a sack of spuds. They both got killed.

As you can imagine, the sergeant's mess was a bit of a glum place for a bit after that, but as is the way of things in the army, you tried to put it out of your mind and get on with doing all the day-to-day stuff that kept you busy. One day, after I'd just mucked out the horses, I was that sweaty I could have stunk the barracks out, so I decided to take a shower. They'd set up an outside contraption that fed a pipe from a water tank to an old oil can hanging over a cubicle made of some sort of grass. When I pulled on a rope, the water tank tipped up and poured tepid water into the oil can, where it poured through holes that had been made in the bottom, and down onto my head. The soap was always carbolic, and smelled summat rotten, but it was important to keep clean; too many men were hospitalized when they caught summat due to being mucky buggers.

I was still drying mesen when I went into the sergeant's mess and shouted to Bally, who was polishing glasses behind the bar. He grinned as he poured me a beer.

"Get that down your neck, Harry," he said, in this thick, Indian accent.

The beer wasn't too bad. Not like the bitter we got at home, of course, but not bad at all, considerin'. They had rigged up an icehouse that worked pretty well, although it needed seeing to regular, so the drinks were allus cool.

I remember looking up at the giant punkah that swept back and forrards over my head, stirring the air on a day that was pretty hot, considering Risalpur was looked on as being a coolish place. The great fan was made out of the usual grassy stuff that all mats and the like were made from out there, and it was worked by a thin rope that went round a pulley-thing and out through an opening in the wall. For the first time, I started thinking about what was on the outside of the wall, so I took my beer and went through a gap that was just to the side of the main door. When I pushed the curtain to one side, I could see an old man sitting on the floor, with his back propped up against the wall. He had his legs crossed, and one foot was pushed through a loop of rope that went up, and through a hole just above his head. His foot kept moving so that the rope got pulled and released in a slow rhythm, and I guessed that this was what made the punkah move in the bar.

He appeared to be asleep, so I looked at him for a while, sipping at my beer and trying to suss him out, like. He looked quite old and I guessed he was about seventy. He was dressed in the usual brownish rags that the peasants wore when they were doing all the grafting that us soldiers weren't asked to do around the place. He had a long white beard, and his head was wrapped in the usual turban that gave his head a bit of a cushion against the rough wall. I coughed.

He jumped, startled-like, and his eyes jerked open. When he'd taken everything in, he said "Sahib?" in a sleepy sort of voice.

I told him there were nowt up, and he shouldn't get his knickers in a twist, and he must've understood English pretty well because he started adjusting the pants that covered the top of his scrawny legs. We were quiet for a bit, then I asked him if he wanted a beer. He shook his head and said it was against his religion, so I asked him if he was Hindu, on account of the turban wrapped around his head. He shook his head again and said "Sikh".

Now, I knew that there were lots of Sikhs in the Indian Army, and they were well thought of as soldiers. I'd seen quite a few of them during my time in India, and they'd always looked reight smart and fierce; not like this bag of bones in front of me. He was looking at me strange-like, as if he were trying to guess what I was thinking, but he said nowt.

I went back into the bar and Bally gave me a puzzled look when I ordered another beer, and a glass of cold lemonade.

"Don't get buying for the punkah wallahs", he said. "They get paid for it you know… three annas a day!"

I knew that three annas amounted to about tuppence, and even in India this wasn't owt to write home about, so I was a bit miffed with Bally when I took the beer and lemonade out of his hands. His real name was Balbir, and as one of the few Sikhs in the cantonment I thought he should have had more sympathy with the poor bugger at the other side of the wall. I think he was about to say summat else but saw the look on my face and decided against it, so I went out through the curtain again.

The old lad looked all quizzical at me, as I handed him the lemonade. He sipped it and nodded, but he said nowt. There was summat about him that made me think he was different from the other wallahs I'd seen around the place. Maybe it was the way he looked me straight in the eyes and raised his chin. I reckon he was proud.

I asked him where he was from, and he told me the Punjab. I asked him what he was doing here, and he said that he was pulling the punkah. I knew he was pulling my plonker, but for some reason I really wanted to know, so I thought for a bit, listening to the punkah rope as is squeaked over my head. I asked him if he'd been in the army.

It was just a guess, and he seemed a bit gobsmacked at first, but then he smiled and nodded his head and said "23rd Mazhabi Sikh Pioneers".

I'd heard of them, and now I was dead interested in this soldier who'd ended up a punkah wallah. I wanted to know how this'd all come about, so I parked my bum on the floor at the side of him. I asked him to tell me about his life in the army, and he did.

Apparently, he'd joined the Indian Army in 1855, when he was 17 years old. By my reckoning, that made him 94! He was a Mazhabi Sikh, so, because this was a fairly low caste, he hadn't been allowed to join the cavalry as he'd wanted and was put to doing all the menial stuff. I knew what he meant... I'd had to do all of it before we came out to India, but at least they'd let me into the Hussars. The caste system was a bit like our class system, but there were a lot more different divisions, and what caste you were born in sort of set out what job you were allowed to do when you grew up. The Mazhabis were trained as pioneer infantry, and his first action was in China. He'd gone on to fight in the Battle of Peiwar Kotal, during the second Afghan War, when the Russians were threatening to invade the north of India. By 1890 he'd been considered too old for pioneer service and they'd just chucked him out. He told me that there had been many others in the same boat, and as he wasn't in a high caste, he'd been left to muddle through on his own, doing all sorts of menial jobs and living hand to mouth, for over forty years! He said he thought that in the next few years he'd be too old even for punkah-wallahring.

Well, you can imagine how I felt for the poor bugger, especially when he asked for nowt and didn't seem to be maudlin about his life.

For the next few days, I got on with my jobs as normal, but I couldn't get the old man out of my mind. I asked around, about whether the men of the old Indian Army were eligible for a pension, or owt, and got laughed out the office when I asked the quartermaster, who I thought might know more than most about such things. I kept calling in on the punkah-wallah, and one day I found out that he was called Ekveer. Many a time I took him some of the left-over vittles out of the canteen, and there he was, still punkahring away as if nothing would ever change. Then, one day, it did.

I stuck my head through the curtain, as usual, and Ekveer was nowhere to be seen. Balbir saw me and started to walk over. I could tell from his face that summat was up.

"He's dead," he said, just like that. "He's dead."

I asked what had happened and Bally said they'd just gone looking for him when he didn't turn up. Did they care about him, or did they just care that the punkah needed working? I still don't know, to this day.

Anyway, Balbir told me that they'd sent someone to look in the stable where Ekveer slept, and there he was: dead. The medical officer had confirmed it and said he'd sort out a padre to do the praying stuff, after he'd got a couple of blokes to dig a grave.

I knew that wouldn't be right and I asked Balbir if there were any Sikh padres in the camp. He said not, so I asked him what we could do for the best and he just shrugged at me, at first.

"We're not priests," he said.

Of course, I knew we weren't priests, so I asked him what else we could do. After a bit of thought, he looked at me as if trying to decide whether or not to say what he was thinking, but in the end, he decided to speak up.

"I think we could do it," he said.

"Do it? Do what?" says I. Well, I hadn't a clue what he meant. I'd never been in a situation like that, had I?

He said that he thought we could do it, on account of there being no Granthi and us being as close to relatives as he has got. I guessed that Granthi meant "priest," so I asked if he was saying that it was alright for friends to bury him, and he said it was. Well, that opened up a can of worms, I can tell you. Bally said that Ekveer was in a lower caste than he was, and it wasn't strictly summat he should do, but he felt bad about the poor old sod being all on his own at the end, and that. He wanted to send his soul on its way in proper fashion. So, he told me what we would have to do, and we decided to give it a try.

Over the next two days we got our heads together and came up with the stuff that was needed for a Sikh funeral. It seemed that they were usually cremated, but burial was allowed anall, so we decided that this would cause less of a kerfuffle amongst the high-ups. We had to tell them, and they didn't mind. They thought it was a barmy idea, but just shrugged and said, "get on with it."

I got on with digging the grave, in between the usual duties, while Bally collected together what he called the five karhars. These were the things that Ekveer needed as his soul left his body. His hair had to be uncut, and he needed a small wooden comb, some clean shorts, a bracelet made out of iron, and a little dagger.

On the third day, we stood together while Balbir said some prayers. Then, I put some flowers on top of Ekveer's body, and we carried him out to the grave I'd dug, and lowered him in.

There wasn't any grave marker: Bally said that it wasn't needed because Ekveer wasn't there anymore. He was in a better place. I tried to believe it.

SESSION 6

On the Road to Damascus

In June 1940, they told us that Italy had declared war against us. That didn't seem too much of a problem to us at the time, daft as we were. They told us we were now in range of Italian bombers from the Dodecanese, although I hadn't a clue where they were; still don't really. Anyroad, we got moved further out into the Plains of Esdraelon, to protect some oil pipelines, they said. Haifa got bombed, but that was about it for us, although we did keep moving around a lot, from camp to camp, before they sent us to Roshpinna, on the Syrian border. It turned out they thought the Eyeties might want to get hold of Syria and Lebanon, so in late June 1941 we rode across the border and took over Kuneitra, in a high valley on the Golan Heights. On the road to Damascus we were, like Saul in the Bible.

By tab-hanging on the radio, we'd heard a bit about what Hitler had done in France, and we knew what Vichy was. Well, the Vichy French were pretty much in charge where we were. Jabal al-Druze means Mountain of the Druze, and the Druze were a Syrian tribe back then. Perhaps they still are, I dunno. Anyroad, the French were in charge and the main Vichy garrison was in the town of Ezraa. That's where we got sent, to sort the buggers out.

Not long after we got there, I was sent on a patrol outside Ezraa, under the command of Lieutenant Bruce Hobbs, who later became a big mukka of mine. Bruce was born in New York and ended up in the Yorkshire Dragoons; funny that, don't you think? Back in 1938, he'd been the youngest winner of the Grand National, and they say his horse, Battleship, was no bigger than a polo pony. That's how good he was, and we were all proud of him. After the war, he became a horse trainer and he used to send me tickets for St. Leger race week every year, until he retired in 1985. Grand lad was our Bruce.

15. British mounted troops, Syria 1941. Keating G (Capt), No 1 Army Film & Photographic Unit. (Wikimedia Commons)

Anyroad, he was leading this patrol when we came across a unit of French Druze cavalry, and we gawped at each other and wondered what to do next. That was the first time we'd ever met the actual enemy, o'course. Well, Bruce just jerked his head in the general direction of the Druze, and we all charged.

It was like we were filming "Balaclava" all over again, only this time it was for real. All of us had rifles, so we started blasting away and they did the same. We all galloped around a bit, like silly buggers and, in the end,

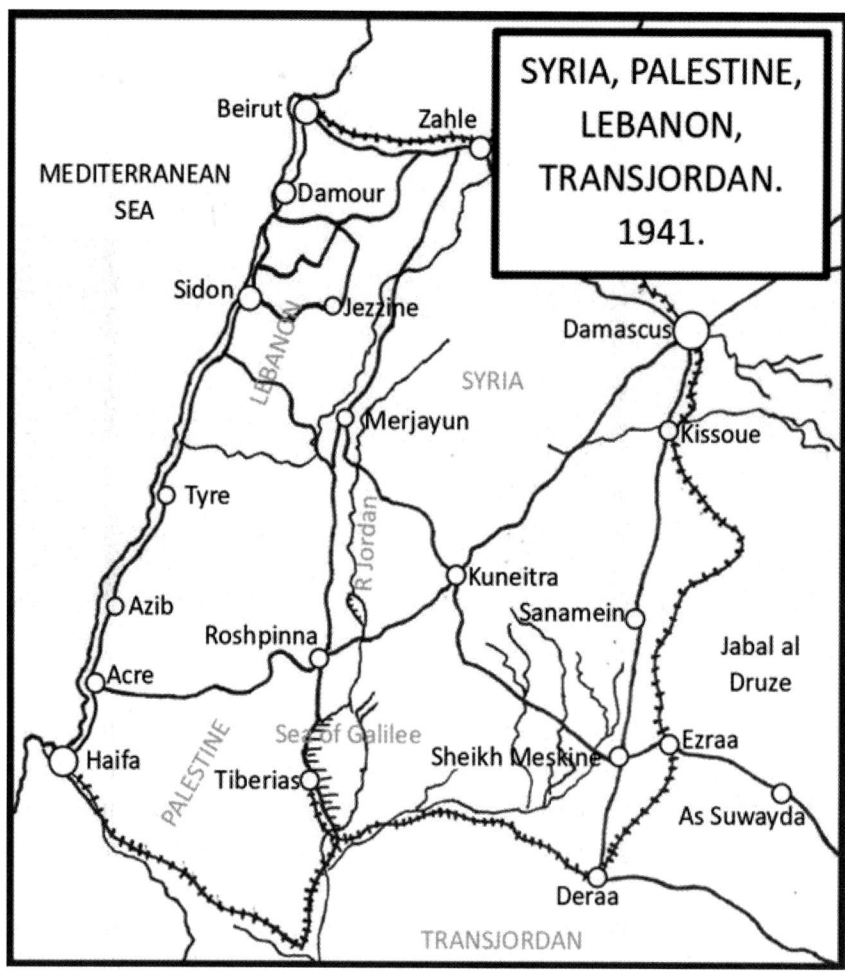

they decided to turn away and they shot off towards Ezraa, like they'd got pepper up their backsides.

I must admit that I'd enjoyed that little skirmish and fancied having a few more, but as it turned out, that didn't happen. The French asked for an armistice, and we led the march on the capital, As-Suwayda. They gave up, quiet as lambs, while we went on a proper booze-up. Some clever sod found a cellar with some great big wine barrels in it and, well, that was just too much of a temptation, as you can imagine. Somebody from 1st Troop, "B" Squadron, who were lads mostly from the Goole area, found the wine cellar, and Sergeant Major Hutton gave us the nod, bless him. Well, we all

16. With Flash, Ezraa, Syria, July 1941. Harry is on the right. (Roger Holgate)

got pie-eyed, and I got totally addled and started laiking about, like a big bairn. It ended for me, so they told me after, when I was dancing on a table and then fell off and broke my arm. I spent the night with the arm in a horse trough and then it got infected, so they dropped maggots into the plaster cast to keep the meat fresh. It took months to heal but it had been worth it. They tell me that our skirmish was the last mounted cavalry action of the British army. Now that's summat to tell your grandkids about, innit?

SESSION 7

Peace and War

In March 1933 we sailed home on the SS Devonshire, and I went back to Hunslet. There wasn't any work there, so I took up the invitation to go and stay with our George and his wife, in Doncaster, where there were railway workshops and coal mines. Georgina took me to a dance at the Lonsdale Hotel, in Intake, and that's where I met your mum. I think we took a shine to each other straight away, and we were soon walking out together. That's what they used to call dating.

17. "The Flying Scotsman" under repair at Doncaster Railway Works 1922. Lyon. F. (Wikimedia Commons)

Her mother owned a newsagents shop on Bennetthorpe, and I got invited for tea there all the time. We used to go dancing and walking and down to Belle Vue to watch the Rovers, but to be honest, your grandma paid for it all and I didn't like that.

Every day I went looking for work and that allus meant a visit to the railway works because they employed thousands. It was famous, that works, because it had built locomotives like "The Flying Scotsman". We used to queue on a bridge that went over the railway station, and they'd come out and pick who they wanted every morning. The queue was allus big, and not many got picked out, but then your grandma came up trumps. She spoke to the Works Manager, after a service at our local presbyterian church, where her and him used to go, and then she told me to queue again, next day. I did, and they shouted out my name. I felt a bit bad, jumping that queue, but you don't look a gift horse in the mouth, do you? So, they sent me to the Wagon Shops to be a labourer.

The Wagon Shops were about two miles away and when I got there, Will Outwin, who was your grandma's brother by the way, was waiting for me. He took me to an office, where George Crawshaw, who was foreman, asked if I'd like to be a shunter. I hadn't a clue what a shunter was, but I said yes, anyway. They gave me a blue uniform and hat and took me out to see my shunting engine. That was, let's see, late 1933.

I got taught how to quickstep and foxtrot and waltz, when me and your mum went to dances at the Lonsdale. I remember Dick Bradley's dance band, and "Moon River" and "Side by side" and "Ain't got a barrel of money". Funny how it only seems like yesterday, but they allus say that don't they? We got married on Christmas Day, 1935 and we had a reception at your Aunty Kit's house, before me and Uncle Alf went off to the football.

On 22 December the next year, our Carroll was born. My wages weren't much to shout about and we used to have to sit in candlelight from Wednesday to Friday, on account of running out of shillings for the meter. That's how it allus was, until the next pay day. In May 1938, my wages got a bit better, and our Pat was born.

One day in September 1939, your mum took the girls to Brid, because your Auntie Kit, Uncle Alf, and their daughter Julie were staying in a caravan there. They'd just got off the train when they saw a crowd of people at the radio shop near the end of the road. They joined them in time to hear Alvar

Lidell reading the BBC news and saying that we were at war with Germany. Your mum told me afterwards that everyone ran back to the train and, when she got home, I wasn't there. I'd gone to the Regimental HQ of The Queen's Own Yorkshire Dragoons, in Danum Road. They were a territorial regiment back then, and I'd joined them after coming off reserve, you see. I'd been a musketry instructor at Danum Road, so that's where I went.

After the Munich crisis, the Dragoons had been recruiting, and now the new lads all came flooding in. We were moved to Malton barracks to

18. Australian Walers. Mail. S. (Wikimedia Commons)

wait for our horses, then on to Louth, in Lincolnshire. As I was now Lance Corporal, I was invited to stay in a farmhouse while we all trained with our new horses. That's where I got Flash. I reckon he was born in 1936, but I could be wrong. He was an Australian Waler, from New South Wales.

Anyroad up, Mrs Ripon, the farmer's wife, looked after me good and proper, and she even invited your mum to stay. The food was all straight off the farm and, by 'eck, I loved her fried-egg butties made with fresh-baked bread. We used to ride up and down all the flat, country lanes, only gentle mind, to get everybody feeling comfortable, but even so, there was allus some silly bugger who ended up in a hedgerow, or a puddle. It takes time to become a proper rider, and we'd been brought up to strength with new lads, cavalry reservists, and officers from The Inns of Court Regiment, so you couldn't have a go at them. They were doing their best.

I had two week's leave at Christmas and spent it with your mum and the bairns. It was hard, I can tell you, knowing I'd have to leave them to manage on fifteen shillings a week from the railway, and £1 army pay, but that's how it had to be. New Year's Day and, Bob's yer uncle, off I went.

SESSION 8

The Last Cavalryman

During the last half of 1941, we garrisoned Jabal al-Druze. Regimental Headquarters and two squadrons stayed at As-Suwayda, while I went twenty miles away with "B" Squadron, to Salkhad. We generally buggered around on reconnaissance in Anti-Lebanon (that's what they called the mountain range between Syria and Lebanon) because the powers-that-be were getting a bit skittish about the chances of the Jerries coming through the Caucasus to get at the Suez Canal. They didn't know if they were on their heads or their arses at the time, what with the Jerries being friendly with the Russians, and if the worst happened, 9th Army, with us as part of it, were supposed to stop them. Some hope, we used to think.

At the back end of December, the regiment moved to Azib, in Northern Palestine, and that was a hell of a ride. We started off at As-Suwayda, thousands of feet above sea level, then rode down into the Jordan Valley, which was hundreds of feet below sea level, and then back up across the mountains of Palestine, to Azib, at sea level. After that ride of well over 100 miles they told us we were going to lose our horses!

It came right out of the blue, and it was like being slapped in the face, I can tell you. You can't be with a horse for that long without getting attached, and I'd been with Flash for over a year by the time we had our last mounted parade at the back-end of February. We were to be the last, active horsed cavalry regiment in the British Army by a few days.

We arrived at an enormous corral, stuck out in the desert. There were a few horses in the enclosure already, and they looked in poor shape. The army was good at looking after it's horses until they weren't up to the job anymore; then, they were just another piece of equipment, like a tank, or a gun. If they were knackered, then they were taken out of service and scrapped. I'd always known this fact but having to witness it up close still

19. Tell Qeni, the highest mountain in the Jabal-al-Druze. Unknown. (Wikipedia Commons)

made me incredibly sad. Flash was more than a bit of kit to me: he was a valued friend and comrade. Standing in line outside the entrance to this desert knackers yard was probably the most difficult thing I'd ever done.

I looked around for any means of avoiding the inevitable, but it was impossible. I thought of riding off and finding some Arab camp that would value a fine animal like Flash. I thought about asking the CO for permission, but I knew it was pointless; orders are orders, and this order was to hand in all cavalry horses for redeployment. We all discussed what "redeployment" might mean. One lad chirped up with, "maybe they might be shipping them back to their previous owners, in Blighty."

I remember Trooper Snipe, who was always a miserable bugger with a nasty streak, laughing.

"Yeah, sure they are!" he said. "They're going to pack them all up nicely, in ships that they need for troop carrying and the like, and send them sailing off into the sunset, back to owners who don't want them anymore."

I could have knocked his block off, the sod. But the other lad, I think he was called Duggins, or summat like that, wouldn't give up. He was sure they couldn't leave the horses out here in the desert. Well, that was meat and drink for a bugger like Snipe, wasn't it? He laughed again, right in the lad's face.

"Course they can't," he says. "They'll cart them off to the slaughterhouse in Alexandria. Yours still has some meat on its rump."

Duggins told him to piss off, not before time, by my way of thinking. I tried to sound hopeful, and I chipped in with summat like, "they still have horse drawn wagons and such." But Snipe was full of himself now.

"Any of you seen any bloody chariots, or stagecoaches out here?" he says, and I had to admit that he was probably right in what he was saying. The war in the desert wasn't one where horses could be used in any numbers, not with the conditions, and the loads of tanks and all. Horses needed to be fed and watered, and there wasn't enough transport to get supplies to them. Stuck out in the open desert, any horsed unit would be turned to mincemeat by the dive bombers and panzers. Infantry was moved around in what lorries we had and had to be rushed up whenever the armour got stuck and needed their support. They could dig in and set up defensive positions out in the open desert, where it would be impossible to hide cavalry, or supply horses. In Europe, horses played their part in the war right to the end, even though cavalry was only used during the invasion of Poland, and by the Cossacks in a few skirmishes in Russia. While we were in the mountains of Syria, and Lebanon, cavalry still had a part to play, but not now. Not now we were fighting on the wide-open spaces of the Western Desert.

Still, I tried to hang about near the end of the queue; always finding some excuse to tell those behind me, to pass me by. I was a sergeant, so I had some authority and I used it, as the corral began to fill up. I wanted to see if there were owt I could do if I managed to talk to the corporal on the gate, when everyone else had passed through, and I kept bending down to do thorough checks on Flash's hooves, before leading him around in circles, as if checking for a limp, always waving the others on as I did so. But the inevitable finally arrived, and I found myself standing in front of a harassed-looking corporal, with the last horse in the regiment by my side.

He looked down at Flash's hoof and bent to lift the leg so that he could see the registration number more clearly. Then, he ticked off summat on the sheet of paper that was fastened to the clipboard he was carrying, and waved towards the corral entrance, where a private was waiting to take Flash.

I asked him if he had any idea where they were going, and he took a deep breath, rolling his eyes like he was at the end of his tether. I remember his words clearly because they stung me as bad as that scorpion sting I told you about.

"Horsey heaven," he said, "like I've told all the others. Are you really that fucking thick?"

I pointed to my stripes and told him to watch it. He didn't seem very impressed. Anyroad, I asked him if they were all bound for the slaughterhouse, and he surprised me by answering in a civil manner. Maybe he was impressed by my sergeant's stripes after all, because after another big sigh, he said that the word was that the healthiest ones were going to be kept as packhorses.

"They might come in useful when we get to some mountains, somewhere," he said, "but I can't for the life of me think where that might be."

He laughed. I don't think he was heartless, just a bit fed up with his lot, and as hopeless as the rest of us. I showed him Flash, and pointed out how fit he was. He rubbed a hand across his eyes and pointed into the corral, without looking.

"Vet officer over there. Checking them over. Go have a word if you want," he said.

I think I muttered some sort of thanks, then quickly led Flash over to where another exhausted-looking bloke was checking the teeth of a grey mare.

He didn't even turn round when he said,

"Yes. What d'you want?"

I told him that the corporal had said he was looking for good prospects for packhorses.

"Yes?" he said. I think he was pissed off too.

"Well, this here's an Australian Whaler," I says, bright as a button. "Fit as a fiddle, and only three years old, and he's been used to pulling carts and the like, in Palestine."

I was lying, of course, and I think he knew it. Still, he finally turned to look at me, and he gave Flash a bit of a once-over.

"Was he a remount?" he said.

I found that this lying lark was easy, once you get into it, and I told him that Flash had been used as a cart horse on the farm where we got him from.

The vet had a sort of twinkle in his eye when he spoke up this time.

"Really?" he says. "An Australian Whaler pulling carts on a British farm?"

"Australian farm, sir," I said.

"Of course it was," he said, and he grinned at me.

He stepped over to Flash and patted him. Flash snorted, and I remember thinking, "shut up, you silly bugger!" Then he went through all the checks that he'd made with the other animals that didn't look completely knackered: ears, eyes, nose, teeth, leg muscles, hooves, and arse. He patted Flash again, this time on the rump, and leaned against him, with an arm over the saddle.

"He'll be pulling carts round Alexandria docks, for starters," he says. "Then we'll probably ship him to Tunisia, if we ever get there. Mountain packs, you know. Can't say anything about after that."

I didn't care. My relief must have been obvious because the vet gave me another smile. A warmer one this time.

He asked me to help him take off the saddle, and I almost ran to do as he asked. My heart sank as he tossed my well-worn saddle onto a great pile of others, then signalled for a private to lead Flash away towards a small group of other horses at the far side of the corral. There was no "goodbye" and no turn of the head as he walked away. I just turned on my heel and ran towards the lorry where the other blokes were waiting.

"Well?" says Snipe, "any luck?"

"Nah," I said. I didn't want to make the others feel bad about their own losses.

Snipe wanted the last word.

"Told you," he said.

So, we set off in silence, and I think we were all ruering like bairns, all the way to bloody Egypt.

547113 Sgt H. Holgate
"B" Squadron
QOYD
MEF
29-9-41

Hello Kit!

Many thanks for the air card, it was quite a pleasant surprise. So glad to see that, at the time of your writing, everyone was OK.

Now, you want me to make it a bit clearer for you as to my whereabouts. Well, I've already told Mary, so I see no reason why I shouldn't repeat it. Well, I am at a place called Salkhad. It's a very old castle, built around 300 AD. It's mentioned in the Bible, so I'm given to understand (mind you, I haven't seen that myself). Anyway, you can take it from me that it's damn dirty. I have told Mary that, by the time she gets my reply, we shall have moved. The same applies in this case, as I am enclosing it in Mary's letter.

You say that you think I am further away than George, or Harry Sykes… well, I don't know where Harry is, but I have just had a letter from George, and he is on his way home. In fact, if he goes on alright, he should be home before this letter., so that says that George is nearer than me. I have made one or two enquiries as to the whereabouts of Harry Sykes, but no one seems to know. Of course, we only have one or two Royal Engineers with us, and I can't get away to find out for myself.

This place is hellish. All there is for miles and miles are rocks and boulders. Really, it's unbelievable and people, I'm sure, must really see it to believe it.

You say there is a shortage of beer and fags? Well. I guess the reason for that is because troops in England and elsewhere, require them, or the main bulk. If I thought they would reach you alright I would send you some fags, but I'm afraid they wouldn't arrive or, if they did, they would be dried up. As for the beer stakes, well we haven't had any for over six weeks, and what we had then was Australian stuff. Now we have just been out and bought some Syrian stuff and believe me, it's putrid!

Well Kit, I could write a little bit more, but I'm afraid the paper won't run to it. It's very scarce now; a pad costs somewhere about 1/9, when we can get one. So now I will close with best love to all at 6, South Street. Tell Alf I hope the beer stakes betters itself in the near future.

Au revoir, goodnight and God bless.
Harry xxxxxx Julie X

547113 Sgt H. Holgate
"B" Squadron
QOYD
MEF
6-1-42

Dear Kit

Just a short letter in answer to the three air mail cards which arrived yesterday. They were dated Oct 24th and 31st, and Nov 23rd. A bit late, don't you think? But, of course, better late than never. As I have told Mary, it isn't through me not writing, that she had to wait nine weeks for news from me. I wouldn't be such a fool as to refrain from writing for that length of time. No Kit, I write every week.

Maybe there were a couple of instances where I hadn't chance to write, but I usually made up for them by writing two the following week. Well, anyway, I am glad she got them when she did as, no doubt, she was heading for a breakdown, by what I can make out of her letters, and your cards.

As regards this J Warren you enquire about, at the time of writing he is at the convalescent camp, and I saw him before he went, and I thought he looked alright. I know he has had a bad time, but I didn't think to mention it because I didn't think you knew him. I did mention to Mary about the death of one of our fellows. He was assistant caretaker at the Central School in Danum Road.

As for the injury to my wrist, I did tell her (Mary, I mean) how it happened when I first did it. Of course, I didn't go into details, but I told her I had fallen on it. Well, I suppose as there is a war on, she jumped to conclusions and now, to top things off, I am in hospital with the other wrist broken. Not bad, considering. Anyway, as long as I don't break my fool neck, that's all that matters.

Oh! Before I go, tell Alf that I think it was swell of him to make the desk for Carroll, thank him for me and say that if it ever comes to the time when I can help him in any way, if it is in my power to do it, he can consider it done.

Well Kit, I guess this is about all for now. Give my love to Mum, tell her I always think of her, and give Julie a big kiss.

Goodnight, God bless.
Best Love
Harry xxx

547113 Sgt H Holgate
"B" Squadron
QOYD
Middle East Forces
11-1-42
12.30 AM

Dear Kit

I am writing this in answer to the letter you wrote on Oct 30th which I received three days ago, also to thank you for the parcel sent off to arrive here for Xmas and only got here yesterday.

You state in your letter that you are all suffering from colds. Well, by the time this arrives I hope that you have rid yourself of it. So glad to hear that Mum is going on alright, and that she is "champion", as you put it. I hope she is getting her little bit of pleasure despite the air raids. Does she still go to the whist drives?

Sorry I couldn't make it for Xmas. You say that you missed me during the festive season. Not half as much as I did! Never mind, Kit, let us hope that we shall all be sat around the table for the next one.

Well love, I was feeling pretty low before I got your letter, as I haven't had one from Mary for over five weeks now. Anyhow, when I read yours, it bucked me up a little bit.

Yes, I heard from Mary about Georgina's visit, and I am so glad to hear that you were all safely in the shelter when Jerry came over. Oh, by the way, tell Mary that I have got my glasses, I may forget to mention it in her next letter. I have had them for about a week now and, believe me, they are a big help. I can sit and read at night now, which is a big help sometimes.

Another thing for you to do, tell Tom Kilmartin that his brother is OK and still with us. I told him about you asking if he was alright, and he says he is writing home regular, so the fault of him not hearing from him isn't his.

You want to really know what I think of the photograph? Well, it's just like all three of them. I won't tell you what happened when I first got it, but I will tell you this; I see it every day and night. I guess you're right when you say it's probably the best one they have had taken. Now I am answering the letter that came in the parcel. First of all, I must tell you that everything that was sent arrived at just the right time. The handkerchiefs I had when I left home were all lost except two so now I am alright for those. Next the hair cream that also came in handy as I haven't had any for weeks now. Of the sweets and chocolate, well I didn't have much of a chance with those before they went like wildfire. As for the razor blades, I had two left out of the box that Mary sent. As a matter of fact, I haven't bought one razor blade since I left home. If you hadn't mentioned the bit of chocolate missing, I wouldn't have noticed and, as for giving my 'Owd Love it… well! You know what I would have said and done. Bless her! I can just picture her face when you gave her that little piece, lighting up as much as to say, "well, it's Uncle Addy's".

I'm pleased you didn't put a cake in as I feel sure it would have been spoiled. Most of them who had them sent had to eat them in crumb form; others had turned green. Anyhow, my parcel arrived intact.

Yes, I did think that Mary did right when she bought Carroll that bicycle. It will help to strengthen her little legs and at the same time keep her out in the fresh air. Not only that, but Pat will be able to make use of it when she grows a little older. That's' why I say she made a sound investment.

I think I have covered everything in your letter, Kit, so now I will continue to answer Mum's little note.

Hello Love!
I do hope you have recovered from your little accident with the lamp post. Please be careful, I know how you get moving when you are out. You must

remember that you aren't a youngster and if you go on at that rate, I aren't going to have you to come home to. So just bear that in mind. Anyhow, I am pleased it wasn't any worse.

You said that you hoped Mrs Gillathorpe's prophecy came true i.e. that we got home for Xmas. Well, as we all know by now that it didn't, we shall just have to do what I mentioned in Kit's letter, and that is _hope_ that we are all together for the next one.

Well love, I guess you will have to make this little note do, as it is now 1.40 am and I think it's time I snatched a couple of hours, so I will say au revoir, goodnight and God bless. Oh, by the way, I forgot to thank you for the card… it's now in the sergeant's mess.

From your ever-loving son, Harry. xxxxxxx
Back to you Kit
Goodnight and God bless, with best love.
Harry xxxxxxx

PS I haven't mentioned Alf, so please tell him that, although I haven't, I miss those nights we had out together and am hoping it won't be long before we have some more.

Enclosed for Julie
To my Little Sweetheart, Julie.

Dear Little Sweetheart
Thank you so much for your nice little letter it was a very nice Xmas box. I hope you had a very good time, and that Santa Claus brought you what you wanted, did he? Wasn't it a little teddy bear you asked for? I hope he didn't forget. Well, goodnight and God-bless, sugar. Be a good girl and don't forget to look after Mum and Dad, also Grandma.

Lots and lots of love and kisses.
From your Uncle Addy. xxxxxxxx

547113 Sgt H. Holgate
"B" Squadron
QOYD
MEF
30.1.42

Dear Kit.

Many thanks for your PC, which I received tonight, so glad to hear that you are all OK at home. At the time of writing, I am in very good health, and waiting for home. You asked what happened as regards the injury to my arm. Well, I guess I was clumsy this time, I slipped and fell back and put my hand out to stop me from knocking my head. No, I am not in hospital now, I managed to get out although I have still got the plaster on yet.

Glad to hear that you had a decent Xmas, of course there would be certain things that you would have to forego now, anyway let's look forward to the next and hope that all this trouble has died down to a minimum, or altogether, what do you say?

Yes Kit, Mary has told me of her bit of good fortune as regards salary and I suppose it would come in handy, she can do with every penny she can get hold of with two nippers like we've got. As regards to the Whist Club and what you say I wrote about it, I can't ever remember saying that I thought it was a beer club, really you both must have read it wrong. I know that Mary doesn't like booze of any description, or the places where they sell it, so I knew that the club must be some sort of women's club. Thanks a lot for your good wishes for my birthday, as a matter of fact I forgot it was so near, the only birthday I can ever remember is Carroll's, and only because it's so near Xmas. I know Mary's is in June, but what day I'm sure I can't even guess. Whose idea was it of adding the little bit on the side of the P.C.? My guess is Mum, I bet I aren't wrong, am I? Well, I guess this is about all this time so I will close wishing you au revoir, goodnight, and God bless.

Harry

PS Give my love to Mum and Julie tell them I hope to see them soon XXXXXXX Julie XXXXXXXXXXXXXX

SESSION 9

A Mysterious Compound and the Ford 6-Tonners

Straight away, we moved to Abu Mena, near where the Pyramids were, and we were told we were going to be an armoured regiment from then on. I think most of us were alreight with that, but then they told us what our first job was going to be, and it left us scratching our heads, I can tell you.

Our camp was stuck out in the middle of nowhere and built on one side of a long, straight road that seemed to go on forever. On the other side of it was a single hotel that had a great big painted sign to prove it. To start with, we hoped we'd get a chance to go there for a beer, but it never happened. Instead, they kept us cooped up inside the camp and we spent our time watching the engineers building some sort of compound.

It had great big, high walls that had barbed wire on top and military police in front. The MPs patrolled all round it, and they had dogs that you wouldn't want to run into on a dark night, that's for certain. They were wicked-looking buggers, and the dogs weren't much better, and that put a stop to any notion of us nosey sods having a look-see at what was going on inside, even when all this knocking and banging started up. Instead, we had to potter about, generally doing odd jobs and polishing stuff all the time, while we tried to stop thinking about the horses. There was a lot of head scratching and general chuntering about what that compound was meant for. Some said it was a secret weapons factory and others thought it was a luxury khazi for the top brass.

I got to practice driving a 6-tonne, Bedford lorry that had a crash gear box. It wasn't easy driving that thing in sand because sand meant different things at different times. It could be soft, golden stuff, like you find on Scarborough beach, or it could be razor sharp rocks that could rattle your

20. Bedford Lorry in the Western Desert, 1941. Smith N (Lt.) No.1 Army Film & Photographic Unit. (Wikimedia Commons)

teeth, smash an axel, or rip a tyre to shreds. They taught me how to do a racing change in that lorry, and I thought of the time I used to help at a garage in Hunslet. They'd taught me to drive in an old jalopy, instead of paying me, but one day they brought in this beautiful, red, German Schneider racing car. As I remember, it needed a new crown wheel, and they tried all over to get one; even went to Germany but couldn't get one. In the end, they had to have one cast locally, and then they let me drive her. They packed me in with cushions and, even then, I could only just reach the

A Mysterious Compound and the Ford 6-Tonners

21. Ford 6-tonne Prime Mover Lorry. US Army. (Wikipedia Commons)

pedals. The silly buggers told me to aim for some soft dirt and then change from top to bottom in one go, when I got there. They said its lower gearing would give me more grip and, as it turned out, they were right. I'd been pretty good at it, so now I couldn't see why an old Bedford would give me any problems, and it didn't. Some of the young-uns, though, had all sorts of trouble and we were kept busy pulling them out of wadis all the time. It was a pain in the backside, but there was nowt for it but to keep on buggering on 'til they got it reight. We had nine lorries in all, and we had to get it reight on account of it wouldn't have been healthy, getting stuck in a sand dune with a Jerry tank up your jacksie, would it?

One day, they asked for volunteer drivers, so I stuck my hand up. They say never volunteer for anything, but I was getting a bit bored, so I went with this rifleman to Alexandria docks, where we went on board a freighter and found some Ford 6 tonners. American jobs they were, and along with the other volunteers, we drove them into the desert, where we found some engineers waiting for us. We helped them to knock the bodies off, so all that was left was just the cab and chassis. It was a bit baffling, but nobody was going to ask any questions, so the only thing for it was to drive them into the mysterious compound and leave them there.

The sound of banging and knocking went on.

> 547113 Sgt H. Holgate
> "B" Squadron
> QOYD
> MEF
> 12-4-42

Hello Kit!

I hope this arrives to find you all at home quite fit and well. As regards to that jelly that you're saving for my party, I hope you don't have to save it long. Do you think it will keep until Xmas? I do not for a minute, think that we shall get home before then, probably not then. Anyway, we can only hope.

You say that Mary is saving up at a rate of five shillings a week? Well Kit, that's swell as long as her and the kiddies are alright. Of course, she knows what she can do, and if anything turned up that required a little more for the youngsters, then I know she wouldn't hesitate at drawing it out for them.

You say there is a whisky shortage, but plenty of beer. That isn't too bad… at least Alf will be able to have his usual, each night.

So, Sgt Houseman enquires about me. I didn't think he would remember me, but then you know what it is… once seen, never forgotten!

You say that Pat still insists that I will be coming home for her birthday party? I wish it was really possible, I do miss them all so much and, believe me Kit, when this lot is over and I reach that fireside, I don't think I will ever want to see the seaside for a long time.

Sorry to hear the film show was a flop. I can just imagine the expressions of boredom on the kids' faces, having to sit still in the dark.

Yes, thanks Kit, my arms are OK now, although they won't be as good as they were. They feel like sprained wrists now and I suppose that will always be there.

You say that best suit of mine is worth about eight pounds now? If that is the case, it appears that things like that must be pretty dear now. Anyway, tell Mary she has to put plenty of mothballs all around it, as I want to use it again.

I will ring off now, so au revoir, goodnight, and God bless you all at home.

All my love.
Harry xxxxxxxxx
Julie XXX

SESSION 10

Secrets and Lies

We used half an empty petrol can when we wanted to mash the tea. They were half filled with sand and then the sand was soaked with petrol and set on fire. We cut another can in two and used the bottom two-thirds as a kettle, then we put the other third on top and used it as a frying pan, with a knob of margarine in it, although we also used the sides of tanks to fry eggs, it was that hot. When the kettle boiled, we chucked our hard tack biscuits into the frying pan and then smeared them with the thick jam that we were issued with. We mashed the tea and it tasted of petrol, but we never batted an eyelid at that.

The bloody weather was appalling. At night it was fair parky, and I managed to scrounge a tanker's gansey that had wool on the inside and leather on the outside. That kept me quite snug when it got nippy, but in daylight hours it was allus baking hot and there wasn't often much breeze. When there *was* a breeze, it made things bearable, unless it was a khamaseen, and then it was bloody murder.

Khamaseen's an Arab word that means "fifty," and that's because they allus seem to blow over Egypt during a fifty-day period in spring. They're hot, dry, and blinding, and they come out of nowhere and blast you at about 90 miles an hour. I heard that they reckoned a khamaseen parted the Red Sea in the Bible, and I can believe it. When one of them starts up everything else stops: walking, driving, eating, sleeping, the war, everything. You can't see, and if you try to do it without goggles, you're bound to get an eyeful of grit that burns like hell and can even blind you, permanently. It blasts through your clothes, and you get a mouthful, even if you wrap a scarf round your neck and face. All we could do was get in, or behind, a lorry and stay there for the duration, and that could be hours. I went through a few of these storms and it's hard to describe the misery they caused.

Then there were flies, so many flies. And big 'uns too. They were everywhere: in your snap, in your eyes, in your ears, up your nose and in your mouth. They landed on corpses and tormented the life out of the horses. Never mind the scorpions, the flies were worse, I'm telling you. You just try having a dump in a cloud of them and you'll know what I mean.

Anyroad up, the banging in our compound went on for days, and while we waited for them to sort themselves out, we used to go for walks down the coast road, where we saw loads of artillery pieces pointing out to sea. Only they weren't artillery pieces, they were wooden dummies. We hadn't got enough of the real things, you see? From ground level they looked ridiculous, but they might've fooled Jerry aircraft, at a pinch.

We helped to build dummy tanks and a wooden loco that moved up and down a length of track and looked like it was loading and unloading gear all the time. They rigged up some sort of gearing that made it look like it was chugging-out smoke when they set fire to some oily rags stuffed inside, and a lorry pulled it along. Well, I reckoned it might fool a blind man, on a galloping horse, at midnight, but the Jerries? Not a chance!

22. The framework of a dummy tank under construction at the Middle East School of Camouflage in the Western Desert, 1942. Leet, G. (Capt.), British Army. (Wikimedia Commons)

I know for a fact that I wasn't the only one who was unimpressed. One day we were mucking about near the loco, hauling some gear around to make the scene look more convincing, when we heard an aircraft. We could recognize all the different engine sounds by now and I knew that this was a Messerschmitt 109 coming at us. We all dived for cover, and seconds later, we heard a bomb coming down as the Jerry shot overhead and disappeared. When there was no explosion, we all went to get a closer look at the bomb. We could see that it was made of wood and had a siren thing attached, to do all the screaming. As we took this in, the bloody Jerry came roaring back, but this time nobody ducked. We all stood there, like statues, as he came down low and waggled his wings at us. I don't think any of us liked him taking the mickey like that, but a few laughed at it anyway. Cocky beggar!

The Redcaps checked our passes when we finally got called into the compound and could see what they'd done to our American lorries. They'd used scaffolding and canvas and stuck a couple of pipes out of the front of each of them, so that they all looked like Honey tanks. If it hadn't been so scary, it would've been hilarious. We'd been training for two months on things like driving, signalling, and other skills that an armoured unit was supposed to have, because they'd said we were going to be an armoured regiment. Now, here we were, driving canvas tanks out of the compound, and into the open desert. I remember feeling a bit depressed, as well as worried.

We weren't expected to take on German or Italian tanks, of course, we still had enough tanks to do that during the day, but those proper tanks had to come in at night, to refuel and sleep and the like, and that's when we had to replace them. They didn't expect any trouble at night, and if there was, they thought that we could hide in the darkness. So, they gave us some coordinates and we were told to leaguer during the day and keep strict radio silence.

That first night we found navigation point number 3, camouflaged up, and waited. The real tanks came back before dawn, and we moved to our next navigation point and camouflaged up, again. We had a Bren gun carrier that could make, what looked like, tank tracks and cover up tyre marks at the same time. For a few days, it seemed to work alright, but then we got caught out, and it wasn't pretty. The real tanks were late getting back, and as the sun started to come up, Italian aircraft came up with it. We all tried to run for cover, and they fired their cannons at us. Well, you can imagine what armour-piercing shells can do to canvas tanks, can't you? We lost some good lads that night.

We watched our lot going east in a massive column. Back in our lorries, we had to meet up with the tanks at an assigned point so that we could supply them with water, food, ammunition, and petrol.

We eventually reached a supply point that was at the end of a long straight road that led into Tobruk. The Australians had taken Tobruk from the Italians, and that was important because it was one of the few harbours where supplies could be brought in. That's why the Eyeties wanted it.

Anyroad, while we were resupplying some tanks, I got talking to a sergeant who'd just come out of Tobruk, and he told me that the Royal Engineers were trying to keep the harbour area open so that supply ships could get in. My mate from Doncaster, Harry Sykes, was with those engineers and I thought I'd take a ride into town, to see if I could find him. While my lot were taking a breather, I took the jeep and drove past the Aussies who were walking into the city. I could see black smoke coming from the harbour area, but the outskirts weren't too bad. As I got closer, I could see what damage the bombs had done to the harbour. It was blocked by two sunken ships, and some small boats were going backards and forrards, carrying some engineers who looked like they were taking the ships apart. I stopped a sapper and asked if he knew Harry Sykes. It was a long shot, and I was surprised when he grunted and pointed to what looked like a smashed-up warehouse. I remember the shafts of sunlight coming through the great holes in the roof, and the swirling clouds of dust that made it almost impossible to see. I pulled on my goggles and searched all the rooms that made up one side of the warehouse, but there was no Harry; in fact, there was nobody at all. Having seen all the chaos in the town, I reckoned that it would be impossible to find him in the time I had left, so I walked back to the jeep, intending to drive back to my unit.

Then I smelled baking bread, and I found a building where a sergeant was kneading dough on a stone table. I asked him for some of his bread and he told me to piss off, so I offered him a couple of packets of fags and he gave in. I chucked them in the jeep and drove back along the now empty road, to the supply point. There was nobody there.

23. A Stuart tank being refuelled from a fuel bowser outside Sidi Barrani, 1942. Mott (Sgt), No 1 Army Film & Photographic Unit. (Wikimedia Commons)

I could hear artillery fire coming from some nearby hills and I drove towards them until I could see our lorries heading for the next supply point, which was now very close to being on the front line, as the Jerries advanced along the coast. I went tear-arsing after them and told them all to get the hell out of it, so we turned round and headed after our main army, as it retreated east.

We got badly shot up, and the Eyeties and Jerries took Tobruk. I told one of our officers about how I'd driven back from the town, and he told me that I must have driven through the whole Afrika Korps. Funny, but I hadn't seen a soul.

At Gazala we were ordered to join up with a load of other units in a sort of defensive box that some silly sod had christened "Knightsbridge". Exactly what our lot were supposed to do in a defensive box, I hadn't a clue, and neither did anyone else, as it turned out. We busied ourselves digging holes and delivering what stores we had left, to the infantry and artillery wallahs that had found themselves stuck here too, but when the enemy attacked, we were all at sea. The light anti-tank guns we had, seemed like peashooters, as we tried to fight off the masses of tanks that came tear-arsing out of the desert, but somehow, we managed to turn them away. We thought we'd had a bit of a miracle, but it wasn't to be. The tanks had just veered round us, and we could see that they were pouring around both sides of Knightsbridge. The order to get the hell out of it came through pretty sharpish, and we didn't let the high-ups down.

24. An RAF Lysander flies over a convoy of lorries during the retreat into Egypt, 26th June 1942. Chetwyn (Sgt), Fox (Sgt), No 1 Army Film & Photographic Unit. (Wikimedia Commons)

Packed with all the infantry and towing the anti-tank guns, we shot out of there like the clappers. Every so often, we had to stop to get out the Jerry cans and refuel. That's when the infantry lads jumped out to set up their guns and try to keep the Jerries off our backs. On a few occasions we had to fight some enemy units that had managed to get in front of us. We didn't have many tanks, and it was touch and go sometimes, whether we were going to get through, or whether there would be much left of us even if we did, but somehow, we managed it.

After we finally broke through the last of the units that had got in front of us, we set off on "The Gazala Gallop," that's what they called the retreat to El Alamein, where we made a stand between the sea and the Qattara depression: a sort of quicksand area that tanks couldn't get through, and so it protected our flank. From there, our regiment went back to Cairo and joined "Delta Force," who were supposed to be the last line of defence between the Afrika Korps and Alexandria, Cairo, the Middle East oilfields and God knows what else. Maybe even India.

I found out later, that Harry Sykes had been taken prisoner.

547113 Sgt. H. Holgate
"B" Squadron
QOYD
MEF
25-7-42

Hello Kit!

I am writing in answer to your many letter cards I have received. I really have been busy up to now and, having a bit of time on my hands, I thought it was about time I replied to you, so here goes for the first one. Well, this one is dated May 24th and in it you mention the antics of Pat when you and Mary took them to the theatre. I had a good laugh too. I bet you were both having a bit of a sweat when you realized she wasn't with you.

The next query you had was regarding the parcel from the Mayor's Fund. Yes, I received mine last February.

I hope that you all had a good time at Louth. It was nice of them to remember me from the time we were out there training around the farm. Write to me and let me know what you think about the people. You say that

Mary had 4 lads in for a cup of tea, when a convoy halted nearby. Well, that's OK as long as they were cheered up a bit. I wouldn't mind a cup of Mother's right now, as hot as it is.

Today is Sunday and I must get this away today, otherwise it won't get finished until about Tuesday. Late last night I received a chinagraph from Mary, and it seems she is worrying a lot about me because Tobruk fell and she thinks maybe I was somewhere near, with Harry Sykes. The reason is, I think, because my mail must have been delayed, and the waiting for news is getting on her nerves. Anyway, by the time you read this she will no doubt have received quite a few letters, so by then she will have ceased worrying.

I think the end of this year will see Jerry at this end, in a very bad way… maybe finished with. Let's hope so.

Tell me, how is my owd luv? I bet she is getting a big girl now, and when I get home, I don't suppose I will know any of them because they will all have grown so much. How about Mum, Alf, and yourself? Still OK? If you felt as I do right now you wouldn't have any worries regarding health.

Well love, I guess this will have to suffice for now, so once again I bid you all goodnight and God bless. Give Julie a big kiss from me, and all my love.

Harry xxxxxxxxxxxxxxx
Pint of Warwick's for Alf.

SESSION 11

El Alamein

I went to Cairo to see if I could find our George. Because he was going to be commissioned a staff flight lieutenant, he was stationed there, with the base-wallahs in GHQ. I found him and we had a nice afternoon catching up over a few beers. A young boy came up to us and held out his hands. George shouted at him.

"Imshe! Yallah!"

That meant "on yer bike sunshine", but the boy paid no attention. I ordered a lemonade for the lad, even though George warned me not to do it, and when he'd finished it, he asked me if I wanted zig-zig. Well, as it happened, I didn't want him to find me a bint, so I took myself off to some toilets, to get away from him. I put my watch on the side of the sink, while I washed my face, but when I opened my eyes, it was gone. I turned and saw the little Arab lad just as he was disappearing through the door, and into the street. Quick as I could, I followed him, but the last I saw of the little sod was his backside disappearing down a ginnel. Best bloody watch I ever had anall.

We moved to Sidi Bish, near Alexandria, and then to Dekheila aerodrome to protect the Fleet Air Arm base there. That's when they told us that they'd lost so many tanks they'd have to go back on their promise to make us an armoured regiment. Instead, they made us a motor battalion and we got Bren gun carriers, 3-inch mortars, and 6-pounder anti-tank guns. We became part of 2nd Armoured Brigade in the 1st Armoured Division, and then we had seven weeks to re-train before we moved up to El Alamein. I went to the Middle East School of Artillery to do a 6-pounder course, and then they promoted me to Squadron Quartermaster Sergeant.

Universal Carriers were small, tracked vehicles that could be used for loads of things, but ours were specially set up to tow anti-tank guns and to

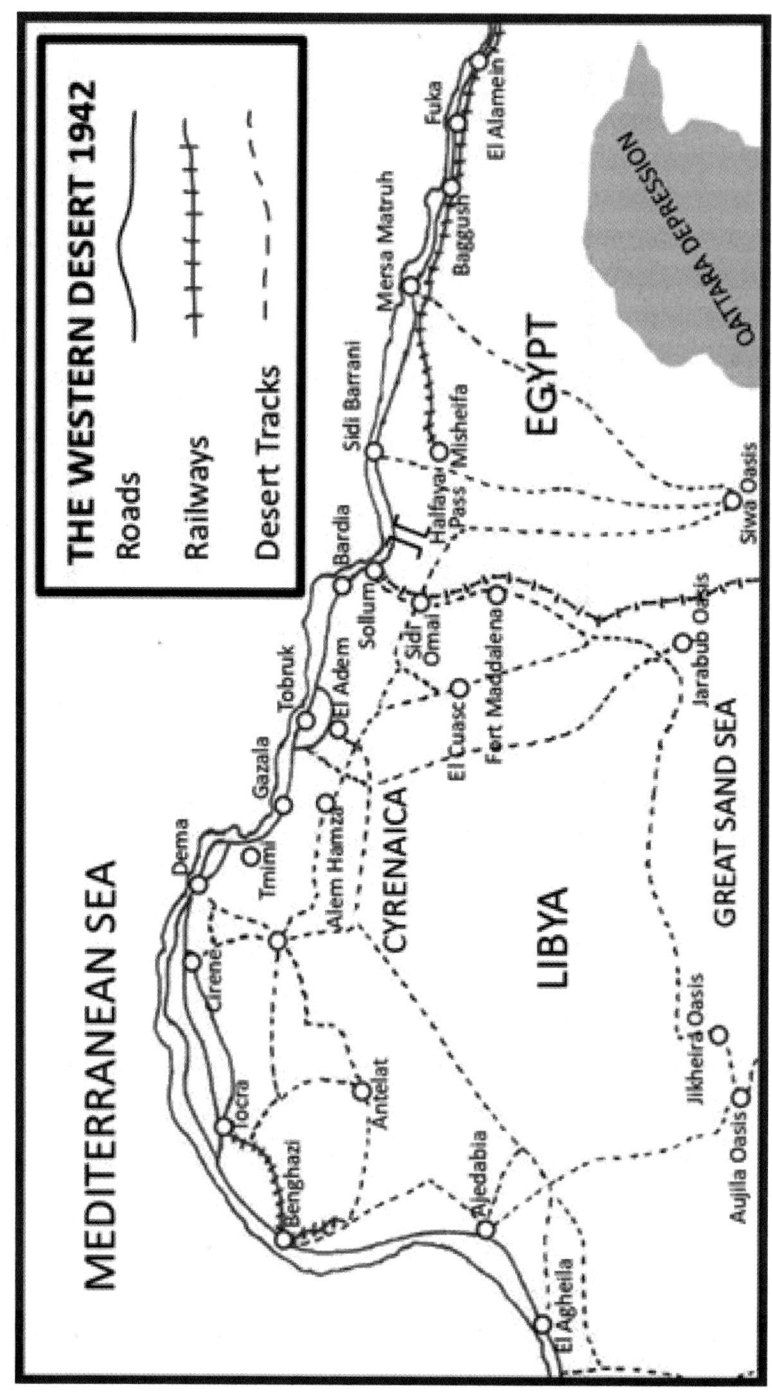

25. Yorkshire Dragoons, Cairo 1941. Harry is on the right. (Roger Holgate)

be a sort of armoured car that was mounted with a Bren gun, which is how it got its name. That was a smashing bit of kit, the Bren gun. It was a light machine gun that used the same ammunition as our rifles but fired about 500 rounds per minute. The muzzle used to get hot quite quickly, but so did everything else in the desert, and we had spares that could be changed quickly.

I remember practicing with the Bren gun and towing the 6 pounder. We had to learn how to unhook it from our carrier and get it into position for firing, as fast as we could. At Alamein, we used to go out every night, and form up in a long line, between some white tapes that had been laid on the ground. We used to move forward a bit, trying to keep the same distance between us, and then we'd reverse back to where we'd come from. We did that for six nights on the trot.

General Montgomery had given us all a pep-talk that went on about no withdrawal and no surrender and all that. Normally, we'd have thought it was the usual top-brass bull, but this time we listened. We knew that we had to stop retreating sometime and I suppose we needed to hear that, this time, we had the equipment to help us to do it.

On the seventh night we didn't stop. The horizon behind us suddenly exploded, like the end of the world had come. The guns banged away until my ears and my head ached with it all. On top of that, I was brickin' mesen: who wasn't? I found out after, that there were over a thousand guns behind us, that night: a thousand guns, firing thousands and thousands of shells at the enemy. I wouldn't have wanted to be in their shoes, not for all the tea in China.

26. A 25-pdr gun firing during the British night artillery barrage which opened the Second Battle of El Alamein, 23rd October 1942. No 1 Army Film & Photographic Unit. (Wikimedia Commons)

I drove forrard and the lorry in front was lit up, clear as day, as the sky flickered with the flashes of gunfire. Gunner Wade looked at me and sort of grinned, or maybe he was just scared. We called him Gunner because he was always gunner do this, or that. Anyroad, the horizon in front was just a great big wall of flames when the first shells landed, and I looked around me to see, for the first time, just how many lorries and carriers and tanks were out there, moving forrard between their own white lines. They were lit up by the flashes that went on and on. I think my ears must've packed in, or summat, because it seemed to go quieter, even though I know it didn't. You know, I could hear that bloody row in my ears for weeks after, but at the time I couldn't hear what the blokes standing between the white lines were bawling at me. I thought I'd done summat wrong, but my head was ringing like a chapel bell, and I didn't know whether I wanted a shit, shave, or a haircut, so I just waved to them and carried on.

A lorry broke down and a carrier hooked up a chain to its tow bar, so it could pull it along. Them little carriers were amazing things: they could drag a 6-tonne lorry like it was nothing and, well, we just couldn't stop, could we?

The sappers had tried to clear our path of mines, but it wasn't easy, and by dawn we were still in the minefield. Us and the tanks stirred up so much dust that we could see bugger-all. We got held up in traffic jams and our tanks got bogged down. The infantry in front were having to go slow and none of the tanks broke through. It was bloody chaos, I can tell you, and we were stuck out there for four days, taking our first prisoners.

The RAF kept flying over our heads and we could hear them bombing, as we crept forward. We saw Jerry tanks coming at us from Kidney Ridge and our tanks went to meet them. I couldn't believe how many there were, but there were a lot less a few hours later. Some Jerry bombers hit a lot of our petrol trucks and that set off a fire that lasted all night so, once again, we were lit up like it was daylight. But we had to carry on; there was nowt else for it.

We got attacked by Jerry and Eyetie tanks and we uncoupled the 6-pounders and blazed back at them. We used to set up in a box of four guns, and their artillery used to get our range from the muzzle flashes, so we had to move about a bit sharpish. We were told that we had to capture an area that could be used as a stopping off point for our armour, which was coming behind us. We were to support a battalion of the King's Royal Rifle Corps, who had the job of clearing the Jerries out. That meant we had to give artillery support, but as it turned out, the KRRC didn't make it in the darkness and the dust, so it all came to nowt. We tried to take the stopping-off point by ourselves, but Jerry was giving us a hell of a shellacking and the going was slow.

I was following Major Glover's scout car at the time. He'd been a GP in Doncaster before the war, and to be honest, he didn't seem to know that much about soldiering. It was just that we'd been in such a state when war broke out, that we'd had to recruit fast, and most of those blokes hadn't

27. In the minefield. El Alamein, October 1942. Mapham J (Sgt), No 1 Army Film & Photographic Unit. (Wikimedia Commons)

been in the army before, like what I had. He was a bit jittery I suppose, that's all.

Our unit were heading for a couple of hills about a mile away and it looked as if the major was going to lead us into a ravine between them. Now, I knew enough to know that it's not a good idea to go traipsing into a ravine that runs between high spots where artillery have got settled in, and these two high spots were blazing away at each other, like nobody's business; British on one side, Jerry on the other. The major just carried on. We got closer and closer, and a few shells dropped into the ravine in front of us. That should have been warning enough, but he either didn't see them, or he didn't know what to do, so I put my foot down and went alongside him. He didn't seem to like it, especially when I started pointing for us to turn round. That's when a bloody big shell landed in front of us, and I turned the carrier and shot off back out of it. I honestly thought that the major was of a mind to do that anall, and I didn't wait for an order. Well, the whole bloody line turned and followed me, and we didn't stop 'til we were out of range of those guns.

The major was the last to get back and he wasn't chuffed. He had a face like he was sucking a wasp, and he started bawling and cursing like a good 'un. He told me he'd report me to the colonel and put me on a charge and all sorts, but after a bit he calmed down, told me I'd been right, and gave me a slap on the back. It takes a real man to do summat like that and I respected him for it.

I never heard owt else about the matter. As it happened, we found another way through to our target, when we got some armour and infantry backup.

They told us that other units of 2nd Armoured had struggled too, on account of the enemy counterattacking. We tried to cut the counterattacks off, but in the end, all we could do was sit there and try to hold up the Jerries while our armour got there.

We squatted in our holes and sweated in the heat. You don't know what heat is until you've been stuck out in a desert. The blasted flies swarmed all over the rotting corpses, and the stink was bloody awful. Burnt-out lorries and tanks and carriers and guns were all round us, but we kept firing into a wall of dust and hoped for the best, I suppose.

Next day, the Jerry tanks came at us again and we blasted away at them again. The tanks that we had went to meet them and there were a lot of

28. A British soldier inspects the grave of a German tank crewman, killed when his PzKpfw III tank was knocked out in the Western Desert, 29th September 1942. Silverside (Sgt). No. 1 Film & Photographic Unit. (Wikimedia Commons)

casualties, but we stopped them. We stopped them alright, and what was left of them disappeared into the dust again. Then, we were told to stay where we were and not move, while other parts of the front moved forward. None of us were against having a bit of a quiet time, so we spread out and chucked camouflage netting over the carriers and stayed there all nicely, as ordered.

It was dark, so we built a wall of rocks and sand around our jerry can kettle before we started to brew up. Our carrier was out on the edge of the leaguer, but we were behind a small rise in the ground and, although the sun had almost set in the west, we thought it'd be alright to light a fire. Somebody shouted, "put that fire out!" but we ignored him. The enemy must have been miles away from us, and anyway, we had a thirst on.

Gunner was posted as lookout, and he grumbled all the way to the top of the ridge, even though we'd promised to take his tea to him. After we'd all had our cuppas around the campfire, Bricky Barnes was sent up the hill with Gunner's tea. At that point, the lieutenant came ambling over to us from the main group of vehicles.

"What you doing?" he says, "lighting a fire, you idiots? There's a war on you know".

We offered him a mug and he seemed to forget about the war. He just cupped his hands around it and sipped the steaming tea. It was turning cold now that the sun had set, and I was glad of the extra layer that I kept in my rucksack; a worn-out jumper that I'd brought with me from home.

We all heard the rumbling noise, and I think most of us were on edge, as Bricky came sliding down the sand dune.

"There's an Eyetie tank over the hill!" he said, all out of breath.

"Bollocks!" said Jocky. That wasn't his real name; he got it on account of always being at the back whenever we went in a boozer, and his hands never came out of his pockets when there was a round to pay for. He was as tight as a Kangaroo's jockstrap.

"Bollocks!" he said, "Their miles away from here!"

Bricky told him to stick his head over the top of the sand dune and shout "Mussolini is a prick!" He said he'd be interested to see what happened but told Jocky that he wanted the money he was owed, first. That shut Jocky up, that did.

We all scrambled up to join Gunner, and he was looking through the binoculars that lookouts always got. He pointed into the dark, and we all strained our eyes to see what we could see.

"Can't see owt," said Jocky.

"You blind?" said Gunner.

Jocky started to tell us all about his eye problems. Short sighted, he claimed he was, but Gunner interrupted him.

Can you see that?"

He was pointing at the moon that was moving in and out of the clouds. Jocky said of course he could.

"How far do you wanna see?" said Gunner.

The lieutenant was a bit pissed off and told them both to shut up. He wanted to capture the tank, he said.

Well, that went down like a lead balloon with us all. Nobody said owt, as we stared out into the darkness. Orders were orders.

Jocky was of the opinion that it was a load of bollocks, and that Gunner was a prick, and the lieutenant had to shoot out an arm to stop Gunner from braying the daft sod.

"What was it?" says the lieutenant, when things had calmed down a tad. He was looking at Gunner.

"What do you mean, "what was it?" says Gunner. "A tank. It was a fucking Eyetie tank!"

I reckon that the lieutenant was nearly at the end of his wick at that point but, give him credit, he took a deep breath and answered pretty calmly.

"I *mean*," he said, "what *sort* of Eyetie tank was it?"

Gunner said he hadn't a clue, and he gave the binoculars to the officer. Apparently, the tank was a two-man job with a hatch on the turret, and one on the side. The lieutenant was of the opinion that we could take it easily. His plan was that Gunner and me should lie down at the side of the tracks, and when the Eyetie opened the side door we'd jump up and snaffle him. While this was going off, he and Bricky would climb up the back of the thing and grab the other Eyetie when he came out.

Bricky wanted to know what Jocky was going to do, and the lieutenant said that he would stay back as reserve, in case we got into trouble.

"In case?" says Bricky, and he was being sarcastic, I think, when he asked what could possibly go wrong.

So, we did as we were told. Me and Gunner crawled across the gravelly sand, towards the tank. It was about 10 yards away and from our low position it looked pretty big and scary. Even so, we managed to get up close and lie down alongside the tracks, as ordered. We could hear the faint shuffling of the other pair, as they followed in our tracks, and when that stopped, we guessed they were climbing up the tank. I had my service revolver in my hand and I remember I was sweating, even though it was clap cold out there, in the desert, at night.

There was a ringing clang, as if someone had banged metal against metal, and I assumed one of the lads had slipped as they climbed onto the tank, because I heard a voice say "bollocks!" in a loud whisper. Anyroad, that solved the problem of how to get the buggers out. The side hatch opened and someone flew out of it like a bat out of hell. I shot out a hand and gripped a leg, so that the Eyetie fell, and Gunner dived on him.

The lieutenant said summat in Italian and banged on the top hatch. In a jiffy, it opened and a man stuck his head out.

"Dint know you could speak Eyetie," said Bricky.

"Picked up a bit on holiday in Capri a few years ago," the officer said.

Gunner pulled a face and mimed, "la-de-bloody-da!"

We hauled both of them to their feet and took away the gun that one of them had in a holster. Then, we started to take them over the dune, to the command tent that had been set up. The lieutenant stopped me.

"Be a good chap, Holgate," he says, bright as a button. "Get inside the tank and pull out as many wires as you can. Disable it, you know."

What could I do? I just squeezed inside and tried to find any wires, and if truth be told, I couldn't. It was pitch black, you see, so I struck a match and looked around. There weren't many wires at all, but I could see a load of dials and pipes and things like that, so I picked up what looked like a starting handle, and started bashing and bending anything I could see.

I was quite enjoying mesen when I heard an engine noise. As I listened, it got closer and closer, until I just knew it was right alongside, and then the engine stopped.

Bugger me, but I knew what it was before I even clapped eyes on it by peering out of the slightly opened hatch. Another Eyetie tank had pulled up about ten feet away, and as I watched, the top hatch opened and two men climbed out. They jumped to the ground and started to light up their fags.

Well, I didn't know if I was on this earth, or Fuller's! I quickly closed the hatch and turned the catch as quietly as I could.

Then, I heard one of the men call out summat in Italian and I assumed he was talking to whoever was inside my tank. Now I was really bricking mesen!

"Hey!" someone shouted, and there was a knock on the door.

Before I had time to think, I heard another Italian voice, and this time it seemed to come from some distance away. There was a few seconds of quiet, and I could feel my heart going like Billy-O. Then someone shouted.

"Get your arms up, you greasy bastards!"

It was Gunner. I tell you; I was that relieved I could have kissed the ugly sod when he opened the hatch and said, "look who's in here, shitting himsen!"

The prisoners were disarmed and we'd started back towards camp before the lieutenant told Gunner to disable the second tank.

"Wazzock!" Gunner said, under his breath, and I couldn't help grinning.

Next thing, Gunner was running past me, like he'd got pepper up his backside. He was shouting "run for it," and out of instinct, we all did as we were told. We'd just about reached the top of the dune when there was a blast that loud it would have woken the Devil. The night lit up like a bloody furnace and we were sent flying over the top by a wave of hot air. A tank turret flew after us, and landed with a great big thud, just a few yards away from where we were.

We all lay there in shock for a few minutes, feeling like we'd been knocked into the middle of next week. The back of my head felt sore, so I put my hand up to see what was what, and found my hair had been singed summat rotten. I was about to ask what the hell had happened, when the lieutenant piped up.

"What the hell did you do, Wade?"

His hair was all over the place and one of his epaulettes was sticking out like a chapel hat peg.

"Disabled the tank, like what I was ordered, sir." Gunner looked as innocent as a bairn. "Couldn't be arsed with all that wire pulling malarky. Just chucked a grenade in the bugger."

Our lot stayed where we were for a bit longer and then we saw a big artillery barrage to the northwest. There were bombers too. It lasted for hours, did that barrage, and then we could see all our tanks, going forrard. There were so many of them, they looked like a swarm of beetles, and the Jerries and Eyeties blasted away at them for ages. It didn't stop them though. The smoke from burning tanks blacked out the sky, and they made a gap for us to get through. Our tanks in 2nd Armoured advanced into the gap and when they got counter-attacked we got our 6-pounders going again and stopped them again. I suppose we probably lost as many tanks as they did, and the sight of so many dead tank men was horrible, but we could afford to lose more than them, and right then, that's all that mattered. War is a bugger.

29. British tanks move up to engage the German armour after the infantry had cleared gaps in the enemy minefield. El Alamein 24th October 1942. Gladstone (Sgt), No 1 Army Film & Photographic Unit. (Wikimedia Commons)

We went forrard again, and it was amazing to see all the burnt-out tanks. They were mainly Italian, and the Italian infantry were beginning to surrender because they'd run out of tanks and ammunition. We did a night march to try to push on a bit, but we got separated in the dark, ran out of petrol, and had to wait for re-supply.

SESSION 12

A Chat with the Enemy

They told us that the Afrika Korps had broken, and we set off after them as soon as we got our petrol. We chased them towards Tmimi, to the west of Tobruk, and on the way, I spoke to my first Jerry.

He was lying on a bunk, in a dugout, behind an anti-tank gun; him and two other Jerries. But he was the one who got my attention. He was propped up on his elbows.

"Ah, Sergeant," he says, bold as brass. "We've been expecting you."

Well, I just stood there gawping I suppose: the bugger spoke better English than I did! He was an army officer of some sort. I never did understand the Jerry army rank badges, and then there were the Luftwaffe and SS ones to contend with, once we got to Italy. They were reight chuffy gobshites, I allus found. I think a lot of them were fanatics, unlike most of the army wallahs, who were in it because they had to be.

Anyroad, I remember this officer was sun-tanned, like most of us. His hair was almost white, he had pale blue eyes, and when he smiled, it was through a mouthful of shiny white teeth, unlike most of us. His mate though, had a face like a kicked-in snap tin, and he glared as if he had a mind to bray me. I pointed my revolver at the pompous sod and told him to get off his arse, while Gunner prodded the other two with his rifle. As they all stood up, I reached over and took the officer's field glasses from round his neck: they were Carl Zeiss jobs and worth a pretty penny. They pushed back the sackcloth that covered the door, and a shaft of sunlight burst into the dugout. It was like the beam of a torchlight, and it pointed directly at something lying under one of the bunks. The thing was bright red and that's what caught my attention, so I bent down and pulled it out.

"It's ten metres long," the officer said. "I was going to hang it from the highest building in Alexandria."

At that point I unfolded the bundle and could see that it was a swastika flag, made of silk and worth a fortune. That made two fortunes in one day! The officer held out his hand for me to shake, and because it took me a bit by surprise, I shook it.

When we got outside, a snotty-looking British officer came up, asked me what I was carrying, and then took the field glasses and the swastika off me. I'd had a mind to get your mum a red silk dress made from that

30. German prisoners of the 90th Light Infantry Division. El Alamein, 1942. Knight (Lt.) No.1 Army Film & Photographic Unit. (Wikimedia Commons)

swastika, and I could've decked the bugger, I can tell you. Yet again, I'd held a fortune in my hands and next thing, there it was… gone!

Gunner was searching a whole gang of prisoners and I went over to help. One of them was an old bloke that I reckoned shouldn't have been there at all, at his age, and as I got closer, I saw that he had summat in his clenched fist. We'd been warned that some of the fanatical Nazis would hide grenades so that they could blow themselves up if they were taken prisoner, and take a few of us with them, so I shoved my revolver in his face and told him to drop it. The old lad was shaking summat rotten as he dropped a small, clay pipe onto the sand. He'd cut off most of the stem so that he could hide it in

31. A British soldier gives the "insult" version of a V-for-Victory sign to German prisoners captured at El Alamein, 26th October 1942. Chetwyn L. (Sgt). No. 1 Army Film & Photographic Unit. (Wikimedia Commons)

the palm of his hand, and I shook my head in disbelief as I picked it up and handed it back to him.

    I turned to walk away, as Gunner carried on searching the old bloke and started to take a watch off his wrist. The poor bugger looked so shaken-up that I told Gunner to leave it. I went back to the dugout to check if I'd missed any other interesting bits and bobs, and after I'd been poking about for a few minutes, Gunner came in and held up the old man's watch for me to take. I called him all sorts, but he said that the Jerry had given it to him to give to me. Of course, I didn't believe the sod and took it back to the old lad, but he just smiled as he reached out and curled my fingers around the watch. I didn't know what to say, so I said nowt.

SESSION 13

The Casualty Clearing Station

One day, I was helping unload ammunition boxes from a lorry when I heard an aircraft coming our way. That wasn't particularly unusual, so I carried on and climbed up to get hold of one of the rope handles that these boxes had. Well, I pulled, and the bloody thing didn't shift. There was a screaming sound, and I knew it was a Stuka dive bomber. I tugged again as the screaming sound turned into a whistle, and the box fell, with me under it. The bomb hit the ground at about the same time I did, and then all I remembered was looking down on the lorry, as I flew over it. The blast took all the air out of me and that was a weird sensation, I can tell you. I thought I was going to die.

The medic came running up, gave me the once-over, and stuck a needle in me. He said I'd got some shrapnel in my leg and had probably broken a couple of ribs, again. I couldn't feel any pain in my leg, so I sat up to see if he was right and quickly lay down again when I saw all the blood.

They helped me to the advanced dressing station and put me on a stretcher to wait my turn with the rest of them. When the head bloke looked at me, he just wrapped a bandage around my thigh, and two orderlies stuck me in an ambulance with a load of others, before we set off for the main dressing station. It felt like they were driving over all the roughest bits of soddin' desert they could find, and we bumped and rattled along while some of the other lads were yelling out and moaning, like nobody's business. I'd still got the morphine inside me.

It seemed to take hours to get to that main dressing station, though I suppose it wasn't that long, and a doctor came and cut my shorts off and prodded about a bit. The morphine was wearing off by the time he really started to get stuck in. Bloody hell it hurt, and I told him so, but he just ignored me and carried on doing whatever he was doing. I think he was

32. Captured Stuka dive bomber, North Africa 1941. British Army. (Wikimedia Commons)

trying to get at the bit of shrapnel, but he didn't manage it and ended up swabbing the hole with alcohol and sticking another dressing on it. I could bloody well feel *that* I can tell you. He tossed some blood-soaked rags onto the floor, as he turned to his orderly and said "CCS." That was all he said, and I must admit, there were a few questions I wanted to ask, but I never had the chance because the po-faced stretcher bearers snatched me up before I could open my mouth. They carried me out and shoved me into another ambulance.

The casualty clearing station was twenty miles away, or so the stretcher bearers told me, and off we went again, this time without a morphine shot. It was sweaty and hot and stinking of blood and medical alcohol, and I threw up. The bloke underneath me bawled like billy-oh, and I can't say I really blamed him. The ambulance crew were American volunteers and they stopped, once or twice, to check up on us and to give out a few more morphine jabs, where they could. They said it wasn't safe to give me any more, even though it had been a few hours since the medic had jabbed me,

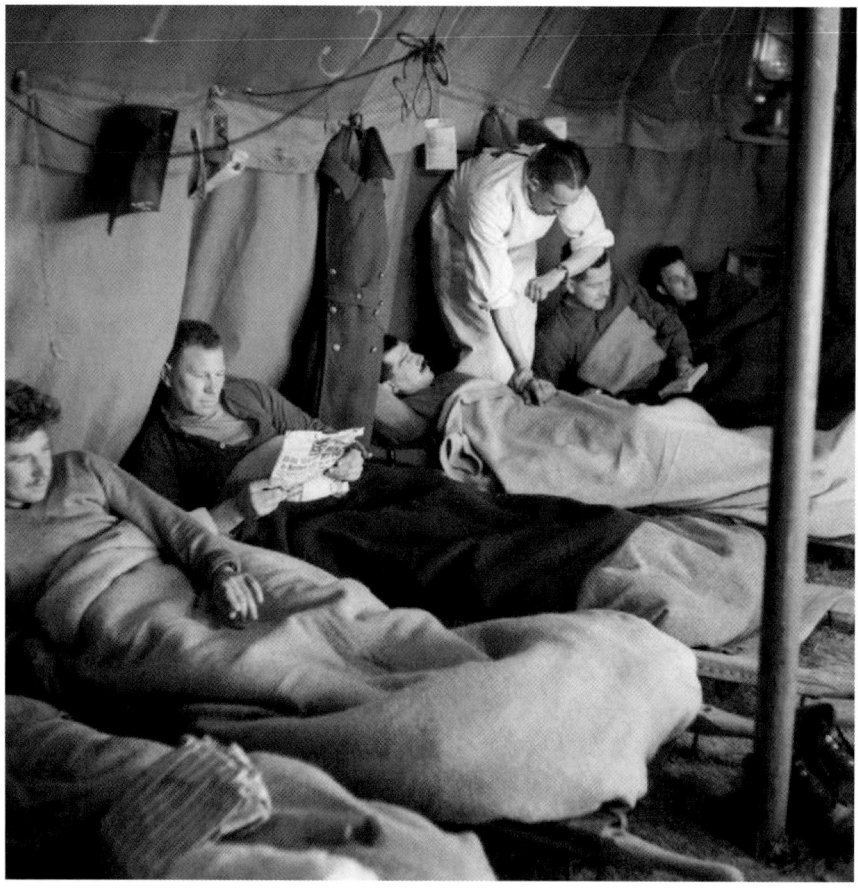

33. A British Army doctor examines patients at a casualty clearing station in Tunisia, February 1943. Loughlin (Sgt), No 2 Army Film & Photographic Unit. (Wikimedia Commons)

but they were proper apologetic about it. Nice lads, as I recall. Anyroad, I just lay back and tried to grin and bear it. I remember trying to hypnotize myself by staring at the oil lamp swinging above me, but it didn't work, and I was pleased as punch when we got to the CCS, I can tell you.

They carried me to another queue, outside another tent, and put me on another floor. Every so often, they came out of the tent and took a stretcher inside. I hutched myself up on my elbows, to try to see what was going on, but my ribs hurt that much I had to give up and just listen to all the curses and screams coming from the tent.

Then they came for me. They carried me in and dropped my stretcher onto two trestles, while I waited my turn, again. I don't think they meant to be thoughtless, or nasty, or owt, it's just that they were up to their necks in muck and blood and just didn't have time to be too careful.

That was the worst time. The smell of ether and formaldehyde made me feel sick again, but there wasn't a great deal left inside me, so I just retched. The doctor who was bending over the operating table turned his head and glared at me, then turned back to get on with doing whatever he was doing. I heard a saw, and then an amputated leg dropped into a bucket with a reight soggy thump. I retched again.

After a bit, they picked me up and put me on a second operating table at the far side of the tent, where a doctor spoke to me in a strange accent. I saw his shoulder patch and realized he was South African. He gave me a warm smile that had me liking him from the off, and when he asked me what had happened, I told him, as best I could. He smiled again and said, "let's have a look, shall we?"

I don't know why he asked me, because I most certainly didn't want us to have a look, after seeing that leg sticking out of that bucket, but he didn't wait for me to reply before shoving his finger into the hole in my leg. I bawled out when he did that, and he stopped straight away, to give him his due. He said something to the nurse, she handed him a syringe and he pushed the needle into me. After that, he shoved his finger into the hole again and I didn't feel a thing, so he picked up some wicked-looking pliers and started tugging and poking around. After a few moments he held up a three-inch sliver of shrapnel, that had a piece of bone attached.

"Souvenir, Sergeant?" he said, and he was smiling again.

SESSION 14

Wide-eyed and Almost Legless

Two days later I was the centre of attention in Ward 3 of Suez hospital.

Gathered around my bed were three orderlies, four nurses, one sister, and two doctors, who all looked at me like you would look at something in a specimen jar. Really unnerving, it was. My leg had swollen up to twice the size and they'd had to take the dressing off because it was too tight. My thigh was black and blue and purple and all sorts of colours, and it smelled of rotting meat, but they gave me some injections over the next few days, and it went down enough for them to be able to transfer me to Jerusalem.

It wasn't long before the leg swelled up again, and they had to pump me full of morphine again. A doctor stood there and told his mate, in a matter-of-fact sort of way, that he would have to cut my leg off. Well, now I *was* in a tizzy, and was about to tell him that he was illegitimate when another voice came from the other side of the bed. This time, the voice was calm and authoritative, it sounded Scottish, and it came from a giant of a man with bright blue eyes and a round face that was half covered by a big, red moustache. He looked down at me and told me not to worry; everything was going to be alright.

The new ward was spotlessly fettled, although some of the plaster on the walls was old and flaking, and it was very hot, even with the big ceiling fans turning. Round and round they went, and my head started spinning with them. Afterwards, they told me that I'd been out of it for three days with a fever, but all I could remember were the horrible dreams. A nurse bent over me and wiped my forehead with a cold cloth, before lifting my head from the pillow, so that I could see my leg. It was clean, pink, and still there. She said something about the possibility of having a limp, but I wasn't really listening; I still had my leg, and that was all that mattered.

Over the next few weeks, I had physiotherapy every day and started to get up and about a bit. I got talking to one of the other patients, who was a mechanic and had dropped a lorry engine on his foot. He'd had to have it amputated, the foot not the engine, but he told me that he didn't mind too much because it was a blighty wound and he'd be going home. He also told me about the other lad on the ward, who was an RAF pilot and had lost his leg in a crash. We were sat on my bed playing cards one day, when we heard the pilot's death rattle. The smell of gangrene hung around the ward for days.

SESSION 15

Via Dolorosa

Major Harris came to see me. He had been wounded in the back during the attack on Tmimi but had stayed with his squadron long enough to see off the Jerries. He said that the dragoons had been bogged down by a great rainstorm and had been told to stay put so that they could be refitted and reinforced. Now he was on his way back after treatment and had remembered to visit me before he left, which was nice of him.

I had another visitor during the time I was in hospital. The padre asked me if I'd like to see some of the places from out of the Bible. I wasn't that bothered, to tell the truth, but as it was a nice day, and as he was a nice bloke, and as my physiotherapist said it would do me good, I said I'd go. The padre got me a replacement uniform, and it was probably new because it smelled nice, and it was a pretty good fit too.

Off we went, into the packed streets, and it was hard going, what with me being on crutches, but we finally came to a chapel and joined the queue to go in. The waiting people were mostly civvies, but there were a few soldiers among them, and I could see from their shoulder flashes that they were from all over the place: Australia, South Africa, New Zealand, India, Poland, and a lot more. Bloody amazing that was. Anyroad, they all looked relieved to get out of the dust and heat of the street, into the cool of the chapel.

Once inside, we had to go up some stairs to get to a place called Golgotha. The padre was in his element and was pointing things out left, right, and centre, like a tour guide. I didn't have much time to take in everything he said, but I do remember the altar because it was decorated with gold and jewels, the like of which you couldn't imagine in a month of Sundays. I think it *was* Sunday, as a matter of fact, but whatever, I just stood there, gawping at all the gold and the carvings and the lanterns and

34. Old City of Jerusalem. Unknown. (Wikimedia Commons)

the big statue of Jesus hanging on a cross. The padre had to shove me over, so I could kneel in front of the altar with one leg stuck out straight. I thought he was going to get me to pray but, in the event, all he wanted to do was show me a hole under the altar, where I could stick my hand to feel a bit of smooth rock. The Padre said that was where Jesus got crucified and it'd been worn away over two thousand years, by the hands of thousands of worshippers.

Then we walked back along the Via Dolorosa, which is what they call the path that Jesus walked on the way from his trial to his crucifixion, and you couldn't help but get caught up in the emotion of all the people who were walking in the opposite direction.

Back at the hospital, the mechanic said that it was all a load of bull, and that nobody really knew where The Cross had been, or even if there'd *been*

35. Yorkshire Dragoons, Alexandria 1942. Harry is 4th from the left. (Roger Holgate)

a cross, but I didn't know so much and, anyroad, it didn't seem to matter somehow. The belief of all those people was enough.

547113 Sgt. H. Holgate
"D" Squadron
QOYD
MEF
19-12-42

Hello Kit!

Many thanks for the PCs which I have just received. There were six, and they must have chased me all over the Middle East, as they are Sept and Oct stuff. Anyway, I got them, and that's all that matters.

First of all, before I start to answer them, I must tell you that I am quite OK and expecting to leave hospital tomorrow. I suppose Mary must have told you what I'm in hospital with, so I won't go into that.

You told me about Carroll's rise at school, but what can you expect… they call her Holgate! (Loud cheers from the boys). As for Pat, I can guess what she is like… in fact, I don't think it will be necessary to send her to school! What about Julie? Has she started school yet? I bet you have a rare old picnic when you get them all together, I know what it was like when they were younger, and I would give anything just to see them playing again. Never mind lass, I shall be coming home sometime this next year, and I guess you will get fed up seeing me.

I am out of the scrapping for a little bit, but not for long, unless the boys finish Rommel off just after Xmas. You see, I stopped one in the thigh on the fifth day of the push, and so had to take a little trip. I only wish I could be with the boys when they enter Tripoli, which they will before long. As you know, Jerry has got youngsters fighting for him, and we took eighteen prisoners the first morning of the battle. The youngest of them was only seventeen, and the poor little devil was shaking like a leaf.

You wrote a puzzle on the next PC but I'm afraid I can't work it out as I haven't a clue what to do, so I think we best let go of that.

I haven't received the letter with the photograph in it but, no doubt it will arrive eventually… if it hasn't been lost, of course, somewhere in the desert.

Yes Kit, Mary told me about the little sum of money, a very nice surprise, and a useful one too. I hope there are many more of them like that because she deserves them, and I know it will be put to good use.

Now, there you go asking me to let you or Mary know if I need anything. I have told my sweetheart, that if she persists, I shall have to use strong language to convince her, and that goes for you too. Please believe me Kit, I only want for one thing, and that is to get back to you all, once again. As for anything else, we have plenty of cigs, beer, money etc., so please tell Mary she isn't to send anything. It always has the chance of being lost, too.

You say that you had the shock of having lost your purse, but the good fortune of having it returned to you. I bet it *was* a shock, particularly with having the clothing coupons in it. I don't understand the coupons, but I know that you can't get the things without them., so that makes them worth more to you than money, doesn't it?

Yes, Mary told me that you all had a bit of excitement when the plane crashed at the back of our house. Glad to hear the crew got out safely.

Yes, Mary explained why you didn't go to Louth, but I didn't know about Carroll attending the Infirmary with her finger.

You say that Syd Browning has been called up for a medical exam. Blimey! If he is passed fit, it means him going into the army, but of course he will be alright... he may even get to be an officer (no cheers please). What about Reg? Has he been called up? What unit is he in?

Thanks for keeping my place open for me, but you didn't have to tell me that, of course. It's nice to know that you are thinking about me, and that goes two ways. Never mind, owd luv, it can't last for ever, can it?

Well, I'm afraid I haven't mentioned Alf once, but then he always knows I am sitting with him at The Tavern. Tell him not to make a meal of it this Xmas, he is to wait until I get home, then we can get really drunk.

So, once again, it's au revoir, goodnight, and God bless you all.

Mary xxx Mum xxx K xxx P xxx C xxx J xxx Alf... pint of Warwick's.

Harry xxx

SESSION 16

Hear All, See All, Say Nowt

The Mechanic told me that they'd transfer me to the first available unit after my discharge from hospital, and I thought he was just winding me up because he was going home the next day, whereas I needed a few more weeks of physio before I could leave. But he was adamant that he knew what he was talking about because he'd had a visitor who'd told him so. Well, I didn't fancy that, and after seeing him off home, I had time to myself to think about what I was going to do. When they finally came and told me I was going to be discharged, I took the papers they gave me and nodded when they said I had to wait for reporting instructions. No way was I going to do that: not on your Nelly! Instead, I just packed up my stuff and left.

I waited around for a convoy of lorries that seemed to be going in the reight direction, and shouted to one of the drivers, just to make sure. He nodded to me and shouted something I couldn't make out in all that noise and dust. When I didn't move, he jabbed his thumb towards the back of his lorry, so I ran as fast as I could, with a bandaged leg that hurt like blazes, and jumped over the tail gate. They took me as far as Fuka, no questions asked, and at the time I thought that was strange. Having thought about it, I reckon he just didn't care. Why cause problems for yourself by asking questions when questions always lead to hassle? Better, by far, to keep your head down, plead ignorance, and keep your nose out of it. We used to say, "hear all, see all, say nowt. Eat all, sup all, pay nowt. And, if ever tha does owt for nowt, allus do it fer thissen", and I suppose the lorry driver was just following that dictum. At any rate, outside Fuka, I jumped down and sat alongside the road, eating the Spam sandwiches I'd brought with me from hospital, and after a bit, another convoy came by. I checked where they were going, and once again, nobody asked any questions when I jumped aboard one of the lorries. I sat on a great big pile of ammunition boxes and thought that there'd be no need to worry about haemorrhoids if that lot went off. To take my mind off things, I took out the letter that Gunner had sent me, and read it again, though I'd had it for two weeks and it would probably have been weeks out of date even before it got to me. Anyroad, it was all I had. He'd said that the regiment was still stationed outside Tmimi, so that's where I was heading, at any rate.

36. The leader of an RAF transport convoy bound for Tunisia, signals his vehicles to move off from their base in Libya, 1943. Royal Air Force official photographer. (Wikimedia Commons)

The convoy went along the coast road, through Sidi Barrani and Halfaya Pass, that we all called "Hell Fire Pass," and then past Tobruk, and on to Tmimi, where I jumped off and went asking if anyone knew where the Dragoons were. I was sure that they must've moved on and I was a bit surprised to find them brewing up in the shade of their 6-tonners.

Of course, I got hauled up in front of the C.O., who wasn't too pleased that I'd left the hospital without getting my reporting instructions first, but as it happened, the bloody mechanic had been winding me up, like I'd suspected. The regiment had already asked for me back and if I'd waited for my papers I would've been escorted here, all official-like. I expected more trouble, but I suppose 8th Army had more on its plate than worrying about a sergeant who'd used his own initiative to get where he was meant to be.

They told me that Gunner was missing, and I never saw him again.

SESSION 17

The Left Hook

So, we stayed at Tmimi over Christmas, and we did all the supply donkey work for the entire corps, shuffling stores between Tobruk and Benghazi, so that they could keep moving after a big storm had destroyed Benghazi Harbour. I learned that we'd lost 100 men since that first day at Alamein. I still remember so many of them you know.

We got some mail, and it was smashing to hear from your mum, about the bairns and how they were all getting on, but it was tinged with sadness at not being able to be there.

Early in 1943 we got on the move again and went into the line at Medenine, with a view to having a go at the Axis' new defence line at Mareth. We moved up behind the main force when it was attacked by the Italians in the narrow gap between the sea and a big range of hills on the left. There was a hell of a lot of shooting, and we moved up into the foothills of the high ground where we could look down on the fighting. After a while, the smoke cleared, and we could see that our front line had barely budged. The Eyeties had pulled back out of range of our guns and seemed to be pulling themselves together, as loads of lorries and jeeps were speeding up and down the ragged front line, presumably carrying orders and redistributing troops.

I was looking through a battered old pair of binoculars that I'd found inside a knocked-out tank, and I spotted a group of soldiers that seemed to be sitting out at the front of the enemy line. I fiddled about with the focusing thingy until I could get a clearer view of them. They were British, that much was obvious straight away, and they were sitting cross legged, with their arms over their heads. A few Eyeties stood behind them and seemed to be waving towards our lads. They were grinning.

Suddenly, the prisoners got to their feet, as if they'd been ordered. All of them staggered and it was obvious that they were pretty knackered. Some

The Left Hook

fell over and were dragged to their feet before falling again and getting a kick for the privilege. Some tried to pick up the headgear that was scattered around them on the hot sand. The Italians kicked the caps and headcloths away, leaving the prisoners standing bare headed in the blazing sun.

Oh, how I wanted to have a shot at the bastards, but I knew they were out of range. All we could do was sit there, waiting for the sun to go down. Nobody wanted to look again, so I don't know what happened to those lads, but we were bloody fuming by the time we were ordered to move.

Our front line moved forward again but got smashed up by the Italian defence that had now reorganized itself. We were pulled back down the hillside and told that we were going to go as support for the New Zealand armour that was going to try to get round the back of the Mareth Line by looping behind the line of hills, in a "left hook.". It was night, and I didn't see much, what with all the explosions and the like. We had to keep jumping down and setting up the 6-pounder so we could blast away in the general direction of all the gun flashes. Firing blind wasn't strictly in accordance with what we'd been taught, but we had to do something to try to keep the buggers' heads down because they were using these great big 88mm anti-aircraft guns as tank destroyers, and they were bloody good. They knocked out so many Kiwi tanks that we started to get a bit worried.

During a lull in the fighting, we set up our 6-pounders in a box shape, behind a shallow dip in the ground. They were well-spaced and ready to fire when the orders came through to me in the control position that I'd set up in the centre of the box. By now, we had to be careful not to hit any of our own tanks that were pushing ahead, into the blackness. We sent some of our lads out to scout around a bit, mainly to see if there were any abandoned stores that we could make use of. In the event, they came back with a prisoner and a box.

"Where the blazes did you get him from?" I asked Bricky, and I can see him now, pushing his helmet back on his mop of red hair that was always well above the regulation length. His helmet had a bullet hole in it, and he'd swapped his own "tin lid" for one hanging from the wooden cross that had marked the grave of a dead Aussie, in the belief that lightning couldn't strike twice. Anyroad, he rubbed his face with his sleeve, and pointed vaguely out into the desert.

"Over there," he says. "There's an Eyetie gun post with a load of stiffs in it. He was trapped behind this crate. That's how we found him...it looked interesting".

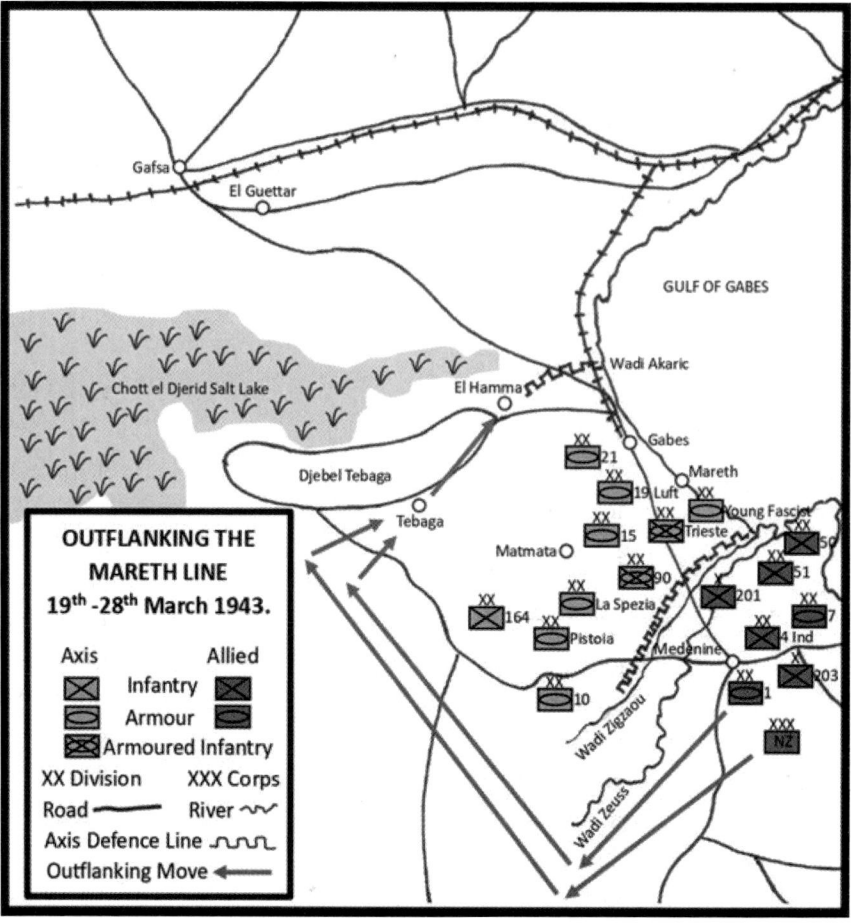

As the others started opening the box and digging out the interesting cans that were inside, I pulled the Italian to one side. The moon was quite bright at that moment, which was one of the reasons we'd stopped in the first place, and I looked him up and down at bit, and asked if he had got a gun.

Bricky shrugged and stuck his bayonet into one of the cans.

The Italian looked up at me and there was a bit of a glint in his eye, as if he was having a laugh at me. I searched him. No gun. Next, I rifled his pockets and found the usual stuff that you find in any soldier's pockets; comb, fag packet, pen knife... you know. Then I found his papers and opened them up. A picture of an old woman fell out.

"Mamma," says the Eyetie, when he picked it up.

"Speak English?" I said.

"No Inglese," he said.

I felt a twang of sympathy for the poor sod, and then tried to read the gibberish in his service book. It seemed that he was Mattia Conti, which I remember because Bricky looked over my shoulder and said,

"wassis name?"

He said it through a mouthful of jam that he'd scooped out of the can with his fingers. He held out his hand for me to lick, but I just shook my head in disgust.

I could make out that Mattia had been born in 1922, in Trieste, and that he was a member of X Battaglioni M, which meant nowt to me. I sat him down in a corner and tied his hands to the 6-pounder. Then we all had some jam with our hard tack, while somebody brewed up.

We were getting along fine when there was the sound of an engine coming towards us, and I stuck my head up out of the hollow for a look-see. It looked like a staff car, though it was difficult to make out in the dark, now the moon had gone behind the clouds. What was clear though, was that the idiot had left his lights on. They were behind the regulation slit in the headlight cover, for sure, but that didn't matter too much because a blind man on a galloping horse at midnight couldn't have failed to see that thing, never mind any enemy gun posts that might have been left behind when the New Zealand tanks had gone through the place.

We all watched as the car drove over to the first of our guns. It stopped, and somebody got out and walked down into the position.

Bricky snatched the binoculars and fiddled with the focus wheel.

"It's an officer alright" he said. "Don't recognize him".

As I took the binoculars back, the officer came out, got in his car, and drove to the next post where he did exactly the same thing. He was inspecting the buggers!

I swore something that would have had me chucked out of chapel. There was nothing to be done but watch the barmy sod drive to the next post, then the next. He was too far away to shout, and flashing a signal would have been bloody senseless. As the car started towards us, there was the flash of an enemy gun, and all hell broke loose. The shells rained in, to the left and right, as they fired everything at us but the kitchen sink. I watched as the first gun was hit and exploded in a rain of sparks. Silhouettes ran through the firework display in panic, and then the second post went up, then the third. This was nearer, and I could hear the screams that came from that place… I still can when I close my eyes. Horrible sounds they were. By 'eck, you wouldn't believe the sounds that a man can make when he's faced wi summat like that.

We opened up in the direction of one of the enemy positions, and I found out later, that the other surviving post did the same. As we pounded away, the shells started coming towards us, but they hadn't had enough time to get our range properly, so they fell all around us. The prisoner was trying to bury himself under a pile of ammunition boxes, which I remember thinking wasn't the best of ideas.

"Get my fucking hands untied!" shouts the Eyetie and, well you could have knocked me down with a feather. I ignored him and carried on loading the 6-pounder as our shots seemed to be slowing up the incoming. Then, there was a great big bang and the enemy gun seemed to hang in the air over an orange flash, before it crashed down in a cloud of dust.

I turned away to get my breath, and then I saw someone coming towards us, screaming his lungs out. It was the officer who'd caused all this, and he was staggering like a drunkard, as he tried to hold his innards in. I pulled my rifle to me because I so wanted to shoot the bastard, but someone pulled it out of my hands and said, "that's murder Sarge!"

He was right, of course. As it turned out, the man fell short of our position, and lay there screaming until he ran out of strength, I think. We couldn't go get him because bullets were flying in all directions by that point, and I don't think I would have done so, even if I could.

As the gunfire slowed down, we were joined by some infantry who'd come up behind us and had taken out the other enemy positions. We went to look at the damage and found six men dead, what was left of them, and all the rest of them wounded to some extent, or other. One 6-pounder was destroyed and another needed repairs that we weren't equipped to do, so we were down to three guns and just about enough blokes to man them. Two Bren gun carriers were serviceable, so one of them had to tow two guns. A tank came by and gave us a bit of chain that we used for that.

The tank commander was an officer and we showed him our Eyetie, who was a gibbering wreck at this point. He looked at the papers and said,

"Battalion M, eh?"

"Battalion M A?" said Bricky, "What's that when it's at home?" He was scratching his backside and looking over the officer's shoulder at the same time. The officer gave him a look that would have frozen the balls off a brass monkey.

"Blackshirt," he said. "Special forces."

I looked at Mattia, right in the eyes.

"Thought you couldn't speak English," I said. "You made a good enough job of it when you were shitting your pants back there".

The officer said that he was probably pretty fluent and was disguising the fact, so that he could pick up any interesting gen that we might have talked about during our tea-break. He was obviously thinking that we might be captured by one of the observation posts that the Italians had left scattered about the place, but as it turned out, us dragoons ended up capturing four anti-aircraft guns and a few hundred prisoners, as we moved through the gap that the New Zealanders had made, so that wasn't bad, was it?

Then we got stuck outside a place called El Hamma, as we got shot up again, and Captain Pettifer got the Military Cross. Two days we were stuck there, getting shelled, before some of our lot managed to get into the town and take it. There were more and more prisoners as we went forrard, thousands of the buggers. They were mostly Italians because they had the worst equipment and the Germans took all the petrol there was, leaving their allies up the creek without a paddle.

We went through Wadi Akarit and turned south onto the Goubellat Plain, which was just one big cornfield, where they'd planted mines as a second crop. Again, we were held up, while their artillery blasted away at us with everything and the kitchen sink. After getting the hell kicked out of us, we were forced to turn back and think again.

We were told to stay put, just out of artillery range, and to carry out patrols that could have a bit of a go at Jerry if ever the opportunity presented itself. Bruce Hobbs got the Military Cross during one of these patrols, and my other mates, Sergeants Harrhy and Middleton, got the Military Medal.

At the beginning of May we went back on the offensive, and on the 8th Tunis fell. The Jerries and Eyeties went back into the Cape Bon Peninsula, and because of it's shape, this was a bugger to attack. We were ordered to attack summat called the Creteville Pass, and this involved us charging across a great stretch of open plain, even before getting to the

37. Crusader tanks in El Hamma, 29th March 1943. Silverside (Sgt) No 2 Army Film and Photographic Unit. (Wikimedia Commons)

bloody place. We were sent off to the left of the pass, so that we could support the Bays as they moved into it. The Lancers went in after them and managed to get to the top of the pass, as the Motor Brigade took the high ground on their right. This had trapped the Jerries, and we went in to mop them up. Then, on 12th May we heard that all the enemy forces in North Africa had surrendered. Perhaps you can imagine the celebrations.

After that, we stayed on the coast for ages and had a smashing time. I suppose we were all knackered when all was said and done. I'd only just got out of hospital, and everybody else had been fighting for ages, without a break, so we built ourselves up and swam in the sea and generally got fit again. We must've been a reight sight, splashing about in the Mediterranean, totally starkers. We'd all been wearing shirts with rolled-up sleeves, shorts, and goggles, for weeks on end, and parts of us were black as the ace of spades, while other parts were white as snow. We must've looked like a load of pandas.

During this time, we heard that the Yorkshire Dragoons had been made into a lorried infantry battalion, along with some of the Buffs, the Foresters, and some lorried infantry from 1st Armoured division. Nobody had liked it, but there it was. We were now 9th Battalion Kings Own Yorkshire Light Infantry (Queen's Own Yorkshire Dragoons) attached to 18th Lorried Infantry Brigade of 1st Armoured Division, which was a hell of a title, by anybody's reckoning. Lorried infantry was supposed to be fast moving, so they could keep up with an armoured brigade and give them support whenever they needed it. Streets and ravines were death traps for tanks, so we were supposed to go in first, sort out the enemy, and hold the place until the infantry proper got there. Then, we were to get back in the lorries and catch up with the armour again. I didn't fancy it, somehow.

At the start of 1944, we got orders to join up with 18th Infantry Brigade. We were going to Italy.

547113 Sgt. H. Holgate
"D" Squadron
QOYD
MEF
15-2-43

Hello Kit!

Many thanks for all the letter cards and chinagraphs, this is about the first time I've been able to sit down in peace and quiet, for how long now I don't know. Anyway, I will try to fill this letter up answering and asking questions.

So, Pat is a schoolgirl now? I can imagine the capers she cuts, and I bet she takes some holding when she gets a little bit older. Anyway, I'm so glad that she has taken to it alright.

Now, you ask if I'm OK again, yes, and back with the boys, what are left. It seemed like coming to another unit, what with so many new faces.

Edith has got another job, and one that she likes. Well, that's alright but I wonder how long she will stick it? Poor old lass... she is a trier. Glad to hear that Florrie keeps getting a few lines from Harry. I bet she doesn't get all the news but, anyway, a little is better than nothing, isn't it?

At the time of writing, I am in good health and sat in a dugout, where it is nice and quiet. Outside, the wind is blowing, and a cold one too. We are well back and having a rest. In fact, you are nearer to it than we are, at present. Does that settle your mind?

Thanks for trying to describe the coupon system for me... but I still don't understand it. You say that Mary is getting enough eats now than when I was at home. Well, if that is the case, I won't worry anymore about that because I always had plenty to eat.

So, George refused his commission because it would have meant him going into an RAF foot unit. The damn fool wants seeing to! Of course, he has a good job, and one that he knows off by heart.

As regards to the parcels you sent, I'm afraid that they must have been lost because they haven't turned up yet. They might still be chasing me all over North Africa, of course, and turn up shortly.

You ask me not to forget to acknowledge the PO from the Whist Club when I receive it. Of course I will, but I don't want any more tears. You say that the last one was pinned to the notice board and that there were very few dry eyes when they read it. I didn't think I'd written anything that would bring tears but, of course, we don't know what they were thinking at the time. Maybe they were thinking of their own sons and husbands.

Now you want me to tell you how I got my leg scratched. I believe I have given Mary some idea and maybe when I get home, I will tell you all about it.

Mary told me about Sergeant Rollinson being a prisoner of war, and I was glad to hear it. We know now that he is safe, and that is better than being uncertain, isn't it? I was with him, or quite near him, doing the same job, when he was caught... he wasn't by himself, either. Anyway, I will give you details when I come home.

Yes Kit, I remember Charlie Bowers. I didn't know that young Davies was his nephew. You want me to give you details about how he was killed.

Well, I don't know, but I will find out and put it at the bottom of this page. Remember me to Charlie and tell him that I shall be round to The Tavern to see him. I haven't made a mistake, have I? It is the big fellow that used to drink with Alf and I at Xmas, isn't it? Or is it the Bowers from the club?

Well Kit, I'll have to close now, otherwise I won't be able to give you the news of Davies. So here goes wishing you all a goodnight and God bless you all at home.

Best love to you all. Julie xxxxx Mum xxxxx
Harry xx
Pint of Warwick's for Alf.

P.S. Young Davies was killed coming out of action. He had a collision with his truck and a Bren gun carrier.

547113 Sgt. H. Holgate
"D" Sqn. 9th Batt KOYLI
QOYD
MEF
14-4-43.

Hello Kit!
I thought you ought to have a few lines from me, in answer to the many I receive from you.

Well Kit, at the time of writing I am in the very best of health, and I hope this arrives to find you all the same. As regards to giving you more details about myself, well I don't think that is possible without giving stable secrets away. I would certainly like to give you an account of what is happening but, as you know, that is just not possible these days. All I can really tell you is that everything is working out OK and that it is only a matter of time before this lot is cleaned up out here. You can guess that we are a lot nearer to home than we were a few months ago, because it only took about nine days for the last letter cards to arrive, and we are well away from Tripoli.

I have written that letter to Carroll, as she will no doubt be strutting around, pleased as punch, showing off the letter from her Daddy. So glad to hear that Mum is doing so well at her whist drives… she keeps on bringing the prizes home. Of course, she didn't have much chance to get to there when she had to run the business. Sorry to hear that Edith has been off work again, I guess it is just a little too much for her and we will all just have to take care of her, bless her.

I have just had my Xmas card from Aunt Florrie. It was sent in November, so it didn't take long, did it? She said she had mailed two POs to me, but I am still waiting for them, and the parcels that Mary sent are still to arrive. I can say that I have them, as I suppose they have been lost… just my luck.

I see that Alf has found a new place to have his pints. The Park Hotel, isn't it? Well, tell him I don't mind where we go to for a beer, so long as we get some. You can also tell him that it will be cheap to get me drunk as I haven't had a beer for months now. Believe me, I will make up for it when I can get some good stuff.

Well, that will have to be all for now. Once again, au revoir, goodnight, and God bless you all at home. Keep smiling, it won't be long now.

All my love, Harry xxx
Julie xxx Pat xxx Carroll xxx Mum xxx. Pint of Warwick's for Alf.

547113 Sgt. H. Holgate
"S" Sqn. 9th Batt KOYLI
QOYD
BNAF
5-9-43

Hello Kit.

Many thanks for your letters which I have received this week, the last one which came today is dated Aug 21st Sat and quite a long one too. Sorry to hear that Mum isn't so very well, I see she was up to her old tricks again, falling down. Now look here Kit both you and Mary know what she is as regards to work, if she thinks it is going to help someone by doing it she will, providing there isn't anyone there to stop her, so it's up to you, Edith, and Mary, to see she doesn't. She is getting on now, and not capable of doing those kind of things, so please look after her, you don't know how much I love her and if anything happens to her I should just go crackers, so again I repeat <u>please look well after her</u>. You are right, Kit, it is very hard to imagine what the kiddies look like, I often sit and try to picture them, but I can only see them as I left them, even though I have the latest photograph of them in front of me. So, Pat still remembers my promise of bringing her a doll home and refuses to have one from Mary. Well, where I shall get one, I don't know, but of course I guess that I shall overcome that difficulty somehow, something will turn up whereby I shall be able to get them something.

Now you ask me to send a request to Hebron Morland at The Gaumont to play Mary's favourite number, OK I will as soon as I have finished this so that they will come together.

Glad to hear that Carroll can help Mary in a lot of things now, you say she can get more sense out of Pat than most grown-ups. Well, if I remember rightly, she always did think a lot of her little sister, bless her.

Do you really mean that you are so hard up? You say here that you could do to borrow a £1, OK look out for it, I will send it to Mary this weekend.

You say that it's in the papers about Middy getting the Military Medal, well I guess when you go to the next meeting you will find out all the news about where we are and what we are doing.

So, Dodd has got home, has he? Well, good luck to him, I think he will need it if he is in the state you say he is, I'm blowed if I would want to come home that way. If it meant staying out here another four years I wouldn't mind so long as I got home in one piece, what do you say? Now don't worry about me, I won't be getting into that state. Maybe my health won't be as good as it was but at least I shall be whole.

No Kit, I haven't seen Kil since his accident, I doubt very much if I shall see him again for quite a considerable time. I do really think he will be sent home.

You say Dr Glover is back in the surgery helping his father, well it looks as though he got his discharge.

You mention something about some more Eyeties in camp, does that mean there is a POW cage near home? It's the first time I have heard about prisoners being around Doncaster.

Well lass, I will have to pack up now, I aren't feeling too good. Nothing to worry about, so once again I say goodnight and God bless you all at home. Best love. Harry xxxxxxx Pat xx Julie xx Carroll xx Mum xxx A Pint for Alf.

547113 Sgt. H. Holgate
"S" Sqn. 9th Batt KOYLI
QOYD
BNAF
6-11-43

Hello Kit!

I think it's about time I got another letter on the way. You say that I had put you all off balance by what I said in my last two letters to Mary. Well, I must say that I didn't think that it would cause such consternation in the camp, as that. Please do not build up too much on it, as nothing is certain these days… but it still goes, as yet.

So, things have altered tremendously at Hyde Park Club, have they? Well, that doesn't bother me any, as I don't suppose I shall ever be a member again. I think that, after this lot, I shall be a fireside soldier and try to appreciate the comforts of home, a bit more. I realize what they mean since I have been out here, and I intend to make up for it.

You say that the children are performing well with their dancing. Well done! I thought they had finished teaching, until after the war. Anyway, tell them I say they have to get on with it, as I expect to see a real dancing troupe, when I get home soon.

You say that Florrie hasn't heard from Harry for quite a long time now. I guess they will have transferred him to Germany, now that we have a good foothold in Italy. Tell Florrie I say she isn't to take it too bad, as quite a few prisoners have escaped and made it back, and Harry might just do that. I hope so.

It appears you had a weep when George came home, and Julie remembered it. Remarkable what children do say, isn't it? And she made you promise not to cry when I get home.

You go on to say that Alf now favours The Park Hotel, tell him to pick me a corner and get it warmed up. What is the weather like at home? It's getting cold here. Yes, Mary told me that they are having a party and that I have to hurry home, as I am the guest of honour. I would certainly like to say "I'll be there" but, as I say, it is in the lap of the gods. Anyway, whenever it is, it can't be far off now, and I would say early in the new year… hoping, at the same time, that it will be Xmas.

By the way, you say you have no idea where we are. Well, I think Mary will be able to tell you… she is intelligent. No offence… I didn't mean to say that you aren't! Anyway, I'll just wait to see how much you can work out between you.

Well Kit, I am going to close now. Before I do, I must tell you I have objected to Mary going to dances. I know she will understand, and so will you when you have read her letter. I will make up for it when the time arrives.

Now I will say goodnight and God bless you all at home. Au revoir. Best Love. Harry xxxxxx

Pat xxx Carroll xxx For all xxxxxxxxxxx Julie xxx

547113 Sgt. H. Holgate
"S" Sqn. 9th Batt KOYLI
QOYD
BNAΓ
26-11-43

Hello Kit!

Thanks for the latest letter card. Neither of you are as intelligent as I thought. You say that you couldn't fathom that letter out, but I suppose I shall be getting a letter from you both, telling me something of what you learned at the QOYD meeting. I hope the major set your minds at rest, did he?

You say that you are beginning to wonder what happened to the voucher parcel, well so am I. It should have arrived by now. Maybe it will get home in time for Xmas.

So, Alf has started warming that corner seat for me, at The Park Hotel, has he? Well, it seems that poor old Alf has got the homecoming bug too. Maybe he thought he had better start early. Anyway, tell him not to wear it out.

You say that the weather is very cold now… well, it is the right time for it, isn't it? It's getting very cold here too. Snow has appeared on the mountains, but down below we are getting plenty of rain. I suppose we will get the snow, before long.

So glad to hear that Florrie has got a letter from Harry… it will have bucked her up a bit, won't it? So, he has been taken to Germany, from Italy, poor old lad. It's a pity he couldn't have got away, same as a lot did. Then he would have been home now.

Thanks Kit, for the parcel of toilet soap etc. I will look out for it. Maybe it will get here as quick as the other parcel. What do you say? In case it doesn't arrive before I leave, I have to tell someone about it, so it isn't wasted. I don't think that will be necessary, so I will just continue to look out for it.

Well, I think that will have to suffice for now. Once again, I will say goodnight and God bless you all at home.

Harry xxxx
Julie xxx Pat xxx Carroll xxx Mary xxxxxxxxxxxxxxxx Mum xxxxxxxxxxx
Edith xxxxxxxxxxx
Pint of Warwick's for Alf.

547113 Sgt. H. Holgate
"S" Sqn. 9th Batt KOYLI
QOYD
BNAF
1-12-43

Hello Kit!
Many thanks for the letter card dated 18th Nov, it found me quite well and I hope this one finds you the same.

Actually, I am telling lies when I say it found me quite well… as a matter of fact, it didn't, owing to overindulgence of champagne, which I was drinking to Mary's health, the night before. What set me off was that

I had just received the snaps of her and the kiddies and I was so delighted, I had to do something. What a shock I got when I saw those snaps... haven't the kiddies grown? Honestly, Kit, if I had come home and passed them in the street, I wouldn't have recognized any of them. As for Mary, I think she has grown bonnier and she looks a picture. I am really proud of her and don't care who knows it. As for that letter I sent that upset her, I am really sorry, I don't know what possessed me to write such tosh. I must have had something on my mind, at the time. You tell her Kit, please. I should have done, only I had forgotten the incident.

So, Major Harris told you quite a lot, did he? You say he told you about El Alamein, and what occurred right up to Tunis. Well, I suppose that saves me a job. Did he tell you that he was wounded in the back and that he wouldn't leave his squadron until the next day? Yes, he had a piece of shrapnel in his back, the size of a duck egg. I was taken to the same hospital as him and, when he got out, he came to see me and showed me the shrapnel. He also told you that I was squadron quartermaster sergeant, did he? Well, actually I am not at present, although I am doing the job. Believe me, I have my hands full at present, what with various jobs which have all come together... and I have the biggest squadron!

So, Pat got her big desk, did she? I bet she's as proud as punch and won't leave it, will she? You say the women at the school think the world of Mary. Of course they do! What else could they but do just that? And you say they are all excited at the prospect of meeting me in the near future. I don't know what my lass has been telling them, but I am sure they haven't any need to get too excited... I'm not so good to look at, I'm sure.

How is mum faring these days, with the cold weather? Don't let her go dashing off by herself, in the blackout, same as she used to. Tell her I am going to take her to church the first Sunday I am home.

So, you know where I am and are settled in your minds now. Well, I will take back what I said about you both not being that intelligent... you managed to decipher that letter between you. Well done!

Well, this will have to do this time. Goodnight, God bless all at home. Cheerio lass. Best love

Harry xxxxxxxxxxxxxxxxxxxx
Julie xxx Pat xxx Carroll xxx Mum xxx Edith xxx Mary xxxxxxxxxxx
Two seats in the corner for Alf and me.

> 547113 SQMS. H. Holgate
> "S" Sqn. 9th Batt KOYLI
> QOYD
> BNAF
> 4-1-44

Dear Kit,

I have just received your two letter cards, dated 16th Dec, and one you finished on Xmas day. Sorry to hear that the duck which was being sent for Xmas dinner didn't arrive. Anyway, it appears you didn't do too bad, according to the latest letter card. You say the price of everything is scandalous. Well, if what you say about the auctioneer is true, I guess some people are earning too much money and don't care how they spend it. I suppose it's the people with their menfolk at home, and not the soldiers' wives… they don't get that much money anyway, to throw around like that. Well, I am real glad you all had a great time. I can see that the dinner, as usual, was too much to run around on, because you say that, while you were writing your letter on Xmas afternoon, Alf, Mum, and Mary were asleep in the big chairs. I remember the times when Alf and I used to walk in around three o'clock time on Xmas day, three sheets to the wind, and sitting down to dinner, then the usual sleep until tea-time.

Yes kit, I was picturing you all, at about those times, sitting down to dinner all around the table, with my chair vacant and all of you wondering if I was going to make it. I only wished I could have done. Well, never mind lass… we will look forward to Xmas 1944.

You go on to say that the kids were delighted with their presents, but that the parcel I sent didn't arrive. Well that, I hope, is another pleasure they have coming. That is, of course, if it hasn't gone astray.

So Jim Barton has got home, has he? Good luck to him. You never know, I might get home in the near future, and drop in, just like that. According to the news today, the Russians are doing very well, and it looks as if Jerry is on the run, good and proper, and if the Hun doesn't pull up somewhere, they will be in Germany before we know where we are. I reckon another four months and Jerry will be finished on that front, and if that happens, the remainder won't carry on, I'm sure. Anyway, let's hope he does crack up quick, then we may stand a chance of getting home. I'm looking forward to that day.

Now you mention about not receiving any greetings from me, I'm sorry Kit, but I put down for some, but we didn't get the number we asked for and, of course, I blew out! I did wish you a very merry Xmas in my letter, but I should have explained about the cards.

You say that I have to give Mary plenty of warning because she is she is going to do some decorating. Well, I'm sorry but you know I couldn't do that until we did arrive in Blighty, because we wouldn't know where we were going when we left here. Not only that but, even if we did know we were going home, I couldn't write and say so, for security reasons. Of course, I would let her know just as soon as I could, after landing.

Anyway, this will have to do for now, as I must put a line in for Julie. So goodnight and God bless. Best love to you all.
Harry xx
Mum xx Pat xx Carroll xx

Hullo Julie!
Mummy tells me that you have had a real good time. Well done sweetheart, and did Santa Claus bring you the bangle? Because I asked him. If he didn't, I shall fall out with him.

Are you still Uncle Addy's owd luv? I say you are, but you had better write and tell me, because Mummy says that you have grown up now and become quite a lady. Have you?

Well, my Little Sweetheart, I shall have to say goodnight and God bless you and keep you safe and sound for always.

Lots and lots of love, and billions of kisses
From Uncle Addy xxxxxxxxxxxxxxxxxxxxxxxxxxxxxxxxxxxx

SESSION 18

A Wildcat and a Stranded Whale

We sailed into the Bay of Naples in early February, disembarked and were taken to a camp called Lammie. After a while, we went on to a holding area in a fishing village north of the city, and we were there a couple of weeks before setting off for Anzio.

There was a shortage of landing craft, and it took a long time to get enough of the sort that could get our lorries there, so we went in before they did. I had a 15-hundredweight lorry because I'd been made Squadron Quartermaster Sergeant and I would need it to go around and sort out the supplies for us all.

We landed at night, and even from a distance away, we could hear the guns and see the flashes, as Jerry shelled the beachhead and the beachhead fired back. Later, I learned that the enemy had a gun that was so big it had to be moved around on railway lines. We called it Anzio Annie, and you heard the bang of it firing, then a second bang as the shell flew over your head. The informed opinion had it that, if you didn't hear the second bang you weren't going to be around long enough to tell anybody about it. They had a lovely way with words, the army did.

When my turn came, I drove the 15-hundredweighter onto the dock, and the others followed me. Thank goodness all that firing had eased up for a bit and we didn't have any trouble, but there were some big warships offshore and they kept firing, so the odd shell came back from the Jerry positions. Next morning, it all kicked off again and some Jerry bombers came over, just to bray us a bit more.

Anzio was about 100 miles behind the enemy front line and, when we got there, they told us what we were going to do. As usual, it all sounded reight simple: we were just going to take Rome.

38. Landing ships unloading supplies in Anzio harbour, 19ᵗʰ 24ᵗʰ February 1944. Radford (Sgt.) No2 Army Film and Photographic Unit. (Wikimedia Commons)

At any rate, we found out that Anzio had been a sort of holiday resort, before the war, and before that it had been in an area known as the Pontine Marshes, where there had been mosquitoes and malaria, and all that bagamashings. Behind it, there was a range of mountains that led all the way to a place called Monte Cassino, and that was where the Jerries had set up shop. They had got themselves into a monastery, reight on top of the mountain that dominated the road the Allies were using to make the main push up Italy, and they were proving a bugger to shift, as usual.

Anyroad, that's why we were at Anzio: to try to get round the back of Monte Cassino and push on to Rome. The town had a small harbour, but most of the unloading was done by landing craft that shuttled backards and forrards, from ship to land. Our lorries were to come on LST's: Landing Ship (Tanks).

By the time we landed, it was like Fred Carno's circus. The beachhead was jam-packed with all the paraphernalia you'd expect after a sea landing: lorries and tanks and tents and artillery and thousands of blokes, all crammed into a space so small you could have almost chucked a blanket over it. They told us the enemy front line was about seven miles away.

We were supposed to replace 24th Guards Brigade who'd been badly shot up when they'd tried to break out of the beachhead. I got talking to a Yank who reckoned the whole thing was SNAFU (situation normal: all fucked-up) and he said they'd been stuck there for two months. The word was that the Guards Brigade had lost nearly 2,000 out of 2,500 men, in that time.

Over a bottle of Chianti (that's what he said it was, at any rate) the Yank gave me the gen on what a cock-up it'd all been. He said that

39. Anzio Beachhead, 1944. US Army. (Wikimedia Commons)

the British and the Yanks had landed in Italy at the back end of 1943, although I'd heard something about that on the BBC while we'd been laiking about on the beaches of Tunisia. Italy's shaped like a boot, and the allies had landed on the heel and the toe. By the start of 1944 they'd pushed the Jerries and Eyeties back past Naples, but then they got stuck in the mountains and the enemy dug in and couldn't be shifted. That's when some bright spark came up with the idea of the landing at Anzio. According to the Yank (who was called Eugene, if I remember rightly) they'd landed and then dug in, because they thought that Jerry would counter-attack. He told me that a Yank jeep had even got as far as Rome and had got back to say that the road was clear, but the American General kept faffing about and the Jerries managed to surround the beachhead while all the equipment was getting ashore, and backup was arriving, in the shape of a British infantry division. By the time they'd tried to move inland, the Jerries were too strong. The Brits got smashed up at a place called Campoleone, and the Yanks got the same treatment at Cisterna. By the time the Chianti bottle was empty, I was feeling depressed.

So was Winston Churchill. The Anzio landings had been his idea and I later read that he'd said,

"We hoped to land a wildcat that would tear out the bowels of the Boche. Instead, we have stranded a vast whale with its tail flopping about in the water."

We settled in and went into the line around the start of March. That meant sitting it out in foxholes, reight on the edge of our bridgehead, and keeping an eye on the Jerries. We had the artillery next to us and I remember them using the new Sherman tanks as observation posts.

The Shermans were better than owt we'd had before: they were faster and better armed, but they were quite thin-skinned, and we used to call them "Ronsons," after the advertisement for Ronson cigarette lighters, that were guaranteed to light first time, every time. More black humour.

Usually we'd sit quietly, listening for any sounds from the other side, but every so often, some silly bugger would fire a shot and then all hell would be let loose: tracer and shells flying around like blazes, and ripping up the remaining trees, where we'd tried to take cover. Bits of wood and rock were as bad as shrapnel, and all you could do was curl up in your foxhole and

40. US Sherman tanks disembarking from an LST. Anzio 1944. US Army. (Wikimedia Commons)

hope you didn't cop one. Mind you, if one of the big shells landed near you, a foxhole was neither use nor ornament.

That first trip up to the front line lasted six days. After that, we were put in reserve for four days, then rested for four days, before going back to our holes. From then until, probably May, we rotated like that, although sometimes we had to sit it out in the line for nine days, without a break. That was hard, I can tell you.

When we were away from the line I had enough on my plate sorting out the inventories, dockets, and reports that were part of a quartermaster's duties. Imagine, trying to sort all that out in between fighting the bloody Jerries! And God help you if your inventory was out by as much as a bullet, or a grenade, or if you forgot to do everything in triplicate. I set up our squadron store in a dugout and covered it with an EPIP tent. It wasn't much in the way of protection, but it was the best I could do.

Sometimes, we were allowed to go down to some tents that had been set up, out of sight of the Jerry spotters, where we could get a shower and a brush-up. Some blokes even went for a swim in the sea, but I wasn't going to push my luck that far.

They tell me that there was a picture house where they showed all sorts of films, some even from America, but I never saw it myself. "The Anzio Ritz," they called it.

One thing I did experience for mesen was the regular broadcasts from "Axis Sally." She had an American accent (and I learned after the war that she actually was an American who liked the Nazis) and her voice was allus sexy and persuasive. She talked a lot to the Yanks, telling them that their sweethearts back home were being unfaithful, and stuff like that: anything to get them homesick and on edge. She told us that the Yanks in England were all over our lasses, and even though I knew it was just her being a gobshite I must admit that it did have an effect on me. What was worse, though, was the way she seemed to know about every new unit that arrived in the beachhead. She'd tell us how many had been killed that day, and how to safely cross over to the German lines, and out of the war.

One day, we went on a recce under Sergeant Major Hutton. At the edge of Anzio there was a place called Lavinio, where there were some houses that we reckoned had been holiday homes because they were all painted pink. They were still pretty much intact, but they'd been looted over the years, and they were a bit blackened with soot. Most had lost their windows and part of the roof, anall. Some bright spark of an officer reckoned that they might be being used by the enemy, as lookout posts, so us mugs had to go and have a look-see.

We half ran, and half crawled, along the beach that led to the doll's houses, then we went in, in groups of three. First, we chucked a grenade through a window, and to hell with anyone who was inside, then one of us went in, followed at two second intervals by the other two. You see, it was reckoned that, in the event of there being any nasties in there, they'd shoot the first man and the other two would be able to keep safe. Simple, eh? Well, yes, as long as you weren't the poor sod that went in first, who happened to be yours truly, on this occasion. Anyroad, I rattled off the tommy gun that they'd given me for the purpose, just to be on the safe side, and the other two took that as a signal to keep their arses outside. When they finally turned up, I was already looking round for anything interesting, on account of scrounging being an important part of soldiering. As it happened, all I could see was an empty wine bottle, so I kicked it. A small, decorated cupboard lay on the stairs, and I checked it for booby-trap wires before going past it.

41. Anzio 1940. Lavinio can be seen at the far end of the beach. US War Department Army Air Forces. (Wikimedia Commons)

The bedroom was completely gutted, except for an antwacky, metal bed. The walls had been decorated with flowered wallpaper, and I thought that must have been unusual in Italian houses, although I'd only ever been inside a couple. The bathroom sink and bath had been smashed and so had the bog. That made me chuckle. Did they think we wouldn't be able to manage without a bog, after all the times we'd squatted, out in the desert?

Then, the whole house shook. A blast of hot air shot upstairs, and I dived into what was left of the bath. I stayed there for a few minutes, until the dust had settled, then slowly made my way downstairs. One of the other blokes, who was a mate of mine that we called Tubby because he was so thin, was lying on the floor, with his guts hanging out. His hand was several feet away, still holding onto an unbroken bottle of red wine. He'd allus had a lot of gumption, had our Tubby, but not the sense he was born with, and he hadn't checked for wires.

By the time the others got there, Tubby was dead.

SESSION 19

Artillery Spotter for the Yanks, and the Bouncing Betties

When we were in the line, I used to faff about taking stuff around our trenches and gun pits: water, mail, ammunition, grenades, socks, and the like. One day, I went to a trench that was reight at the front of our position and saw a few lads staring out over the rim of their dugout and pointing. They told me that, the day before, they'd lost contact with the section on the left, and Sergeant Robson had gone out with a squad to try to reconnect the link. It seemed that they'd taken a wrong turn in all that maze of trenches, and most of them had been captured, but Sergeant Robson had managed to hide himself in an old, shattered foxhole, that just happened to overlook the main road to Rome.

Over the telephone line that he'd reconnected, he somehow got in contact with an American artillery unit, and was acting as a forward observation post, directing gunfire onto traffic on the road, as well as enemy gun emplacements. He sat out there for four days, all on his own, managing to survive on the rations in his pack. The Jerries must've guessed that someone was out there, directing American fire, and they were damned if they weren't going to get him. They threw the kitchen sink at Sergeant Robson, and that's no lie.

The first night that the firing eased up a bit, a unit of Yanks went out, under smoke, and fetched the sergeant in. They took him back to their artillery HQ and he slept for two days, so they said, before they fed him up and an officer took him outside. The story goes that there was a line of great big artillery guns, all pointing towards the German lines, and the Yank officer told Sergeant Robson to "give it back to the bastards". So, he walked down

42. British Infantry occupy a captured German communications trench during the offensive at Anzio, 22 May 1944. Radford (Sgt) No 2 Army Film & Photographic Unit. (Wikimedia Commons)

the line of guns and pulled the lanyard on every one of them. Apparently, his spotting had let the Yanks get Anzio Annie.

Just after that, the Jerries came up with another idea to torment us, by sending over a bomber every night, just as most of us were hoping to doze off for a bit. The single plane would come roaring out of the dark, spraying us with bullets and bombs, and by the time we got organized, he was always out of range and tear-arsing down the length of the perimeter. We could follow his path by the bomb flashes that ran right along the bay. I don't know who came up with the name "Bedcheck Charlie," but that's what we called the bugger, when we weren't calling him summat far worse. Never saw one of these planes shot down, and that's a fact.

Then we were treated to another, new German tactic of planting a special type of mine that blew up in the air. Of course, the Jerries knew what they were doing, because the bloody things were designed to scatter a rain of shrapnel that was no fun at all. When anyone trod on them they shot up and exploded at about head height, and I saw many a bloke blown apart by the horrible things. We called them "Bouncing Betties," which was a jokey name for summat that wasn't funny at all. Nobody dared to move until the mine disposal wallahs had cleared an area where they'd been laid, and that made life just a little more miserable for all of us.

Some nights, of course, the Luftwaffe decided that we should be given a proper shellacking from a whole lot of bombers together. We knew when this was going to happen, because we'd hear the drone of a single plane, flying high above, and then we'd see a bright light as a giant flare floated down towards us, fastened to a parachute. We called them "Chandeliers," and the sods took ages to drift down, lighting up the whole beachhead, bright as day, for the bombers to follow and pick their targets. I used to try to bury myself under anything I could find, but if it was your turn, there was nowt you could do about it; the bombs would smash through any shelter we could find.

SESSION 20

The Anzio Runs and Other Eruptions

The night they brought in Sergeant Robson, I had a meet-up with two Americans in my store tent. They were as bent as a nine-bob note, but that was fine by me, in the circumstances. I had a bottle of Tunisian wine and they had brandy, and I even had the glasses that we'd made when we were in Libya. We'd made them by partially filling some old beer bottles with petrol, setting fire to it, and then tapping the bottles so that they snapped off neatly where the surface of the petrol had been. The edges were smooth because we'd ground them in the sand. Anyroad, after a toast, I got out a crate of captured sidearms, mainly Lugers and Barettas, and they showed me a pearl necklace. We made the swap, and I had a present for your mum. Pearls were better than an old swastika, I reckoned.

One night, in the middle of March, we were told to attack, along with the 14th Foresters. We were given an objective, some bloody un-named place in the dark, and apparently, we reached it, even though we'd started out without a full complement, having been on the receiving end of a proper shellacking before we'd even left our start line. I didn't know where we were, but it was bloody awful, wherever it was. There were gullies and ravines and rocks that had edges like razors, and when we got to our objective, wherever that was, there wasn't any chance of doing any mopping up. After a bit, the Jerries counter-attacked, and there were hundreds of the buggers; SS anall. The two forward squadrons were cut off and then ran out of ammunition. A few escaped being captured and, along with the rest of us, managed to get back to our lines, but it wasn't easy. We lost a lot of good lads that day and C Squadron didn't exist anymore.

The conditions went from bad to worse. We had freezing rain and flooded trenches and mud, and we had to traipse up to the front line every night, carrying supplies. After a bit though, it warmed up a tad and they managed

43. A British soldier guards German prisoners. Anzio 1944. Menzies (Sgt), No 2 Army Film & Photographic Unit. (Wikimedia Commons)

to build some paths up to the front line. We used the mobile showers a lot more, because we were all black-bright and lousey, and there was an outbreak of dysentery that we called the "Anzio Runs".

That sounds funny, but it wasn't, as I found out. I got the runs that bad I could've shit though the eye of a needle, I'm telling you. I got ordered to the MO's tent and he took one look at me and sent me back to Naples, to the big hospital there. By the time I arrived I was in a sorry state, and they poured some disgusting, milky-looking stuff into my mouth and told me not

44. Mt Vesuvius erupts, March 1944. John Reinhardt, B24 tail gunner USAAF. (Wikipedia)

to swallow until they'd got the X-ray machine into position. The barium meal told them that I had a duodenal infection, caused by the water at Anzio, but the doctor said he would soon have me back with my pals and I thought he must be half-baked if he thought that was going to cheer me up.

On my first day in hospital, I was jolted awake by a great booming noise and the whole place seemed to shudder. Nurses ran around in the half-light because the electricity had gone, and a red glow in the sky made it look like how you'd imagine hell to be. They'd told me that Mount Vesuvius had been doing a bit of "grumbling" and that lava had overflowed from it a bit. "Nothing to worry about," they'd said. Now, that seemed to have changed. Somebody near a window shouted out that the volcano was erupting, and that didn't help to calm everybody down, I can tell you. I was on the first floor, and they started bringing people up from the ground floor, on account of the fact they didn't know how far the lava was going to spread. My bed was covered in ash, and I coughed and spluttered all through the night.

Next morning, I went to the window to see that the edge of the lava was creeping slowly forward, setting fire to trees as it came. The doctor, who was Italian, told me that the locals would soon be cutting away lumps of lava to make them into the shape of birds, animals, fish and the like. According to him, they'd polish them up and sell them, like people had done after previous eruptions.

547113 SQMS H. Holgate
Support Squadron
9th KOYLI (Yorks. D.)
CMF
15/3/44

Dear Kit

Many thanks for all the letters you sent during the past few months, I am very sorry that I haven't been able to answer them. At the moment I have a little time to spare so I took the opportunity of getting this done. Well Kit your last letter which arrived a couple of days ago said that you were all OK at home, so glad to hear that. At the time of writing, I am not feeling too grand, my stomach is bothering me a bit, and I am thinking of going sick tomorrow because I have stuck it as long as

I can. I just can't keep it up as all the food I take comes back. Don't go and tell Mary what I have just said, or she will go worrying herself, and I don't want her to do that. You say that Georgina has had a little boy, well I am glad she has got it over, maybe that will keep her more occupied, what do you say? As a matter of fact, I have just had a letter from George today, he told me all about it. He said that Mary was the first to know with it taking place at Stainforth. He sounded real pleased. He went on to say that his commission had not come through and that he was browned off waiting. By the way, it appears that George visited the school, and he went to the classroom where Pat was. She just dropped her head and blushed because she thought it was me, poor old lass, I bet she must have had a real shock, don't you? Never mind, maybe it won't be long now before I do get home. When I do, I shall give them plenty of warning now that I know what will happen. They must be all keyed up to go off like that. So, Alf has to make a chair for the big US Army boss, has he? * Tell him to make it very comfortable for him as this war game is very tiring. You can also tell him that there is a small-time boss here who requires a nice comfy chair to lounge in when he does get home. Glad to hear that Harry Sykes is still in very good health and spirits, it must be very trying being a prisoner of war. When I write to Mary, I shall tell her to send him some fags through the Red Cross Society. It's not so bad if one has a smoke in times like that, I know they came in very handy when I was in hospital. Oh! I have just had a letter from Aunt Lena in the USA. She evidently received my letter and was thrilled to bits with it because she says she took it all round to show her friends. She goes on to say that Cousin Alex from Leeds, chief gunner on the HMS Duke of York, was mentioned in all the papers, his photo was also displayed, and it appears he was one of the crew responsible for sinking the German battleship Scharnhorst, quite a feat what? You want to know if I get any papers from home. No. I told Mary to stop sending them when I was in Palestine, they never used to get to me, and I thought it was a waste of time. I don't get much chance to read these days I am too busy. No Kit, I am not in the same place as I was when I wrote to you last time, I am in Italy now and in action again. I repeat, don't tell Mary or she will just about go off her head. Tell her that I am OK which I am bar the complaint I told you of. Well lass, I think this is all I have to say this time, so again I say goodnight and God bless you all at home. Best of luck and keep smiling.

Harry xxxxxxxxxxxxx

Julie xxx Pat xxx Carroll xxx Mum xxx Edith xxx Mary xxx

(*Author's Note: Alf was an upholsterer at Doncaster Railway Works and made the seating for the railway carriage to be used by the Supreme Commander of the Allied Expeditionary Force in Europe, General Dwight D. Eisenhower (later to become President of the United States of America).

547113 SQMS H. Holgate
Support Squadron
9th KOYLI
QOYD
CMF
22/4/44

Dear Kit

Many thanks for your letter dated 14th April, which arrived here yesterday. Only six days to get here… not bad! You begin by saying you feel heaps better because Mary has just had one of my letters, and on top of that you had some good news, which you say has made you all happier than you ever have been since I left. Well, I'm real pleased to hear that, but I can't fall in with your idea of me being home before you write your next letter to me. Of course, it can be done if you write once a year, instead of once a week!

You don't mention what the good news was, but I think I can guess… tell me if I'm right. "Someone has told you that we are coming home soon" is that it? Now, if I am right, take a little advice and don't believe anything from anyone about this coming home business. I have told Mary, many times, to ignore such things. You believe it, then start building up hopes and, when nothing happens, you feel a darned sight worse than before. If you expect me when you see me, you won't be far out. As a matter of fact, as regards to me being home in a fortnight, or the time you have been told, it's all my eye because, at the time of writing, I am in hospital.

I saw in your letter that you advised me to have my tummy seen to. Well, that's the reason I'm in hospital right now, and I think I shall be in for quite a spell, unless they patch my tummy up a bit. I hope this time will cure me for good, as you know I have had two bad spells with it and, both times, I was supposed to be cured. Well, this time I have been thoroughly overhauled and X-rayed, and I do believe that I shall get the right treatment this time.

It appears that Mary is getting on famous with her job. I'm real glad… it's a job that will occupy her mind a bit more because she loves the kiddies. I can just picture her at that school, parading 160 kiddies and inspecting their little heads, before meals, then sitting down at the piano after the meal is over and hearing all them singing. I bet she is in her element.

You say that Mary is looking out for that cheque I sent. Well, it should have arrived by now, as it is a month ago since I sent it off! Of course, it may be delayed at this end, owing to the position we are in. You say that it will look better in the bank than in the till. Of course it will…that's where I intended it to go unless, of course, Mary needed it.

Well, I guess this is the limit this time, so once again I will wish you all goodnight and God bless.

All my love
Harry xxxxxxxxxxxxxxx
Pat xxx Julie xxx Carroll xxx Mum xxx Edith xxx

SESSION 21

The Caesar Line, a Trip to Rome, and a Pig

When I got back to the regiment we had a lot of new faces, straight out of England and bright-eyed and bushy-tailed, bless 'em. They'd learn, I thought. We were up to strength again and had a new colonel from the Lancashire Fusiliers. The supply store had been flattened by a shell and I had to report, "entire stock – LEA" which meant Lost Enemy Action. That sort of got me out of any possible questions about the disappearance of a crate of Lugers and Barettas. They told me that the Poles had taken Monte Cassino, and now we could have a two-pronged push to Rome.

It started with an artillery barrage, as usual, and then we watched the ground attack aircraft go in to support our advancing ground forces before it was our turn. As part of 1st Infantry Division, we headed towards Carraceto Station. The Jerries fought like they always did, and we took another shellacking, but there was no stopping us this time. At one point, when we were attacking at night, I saw one of our troopers jump out of the lorry in front of me and dive into a ditch at the side of the road. I wondered what the hell he was doing and jumped out of my 15-hundredweighter to find out. He pointed to some trees just a bit ahead, and he must've had eyes like a hawk because I'd never have seen that tank in a month of Sundays. They were probably waiting for us to get past them, so that they could shoot us up the backside, and then we'd have really been up the creek without a paddle. We had a new PIAT in the lorry, that's Projector, Infantry, Anti-Tank, although it was really an Infantry Anti-Tank Projector, but I suppose they couldn't make up a clever acronym that way. Anyroad, he went back for it. He was one of the new lads and I can't, for the life of me, remember his name.

The Last Cavalryman

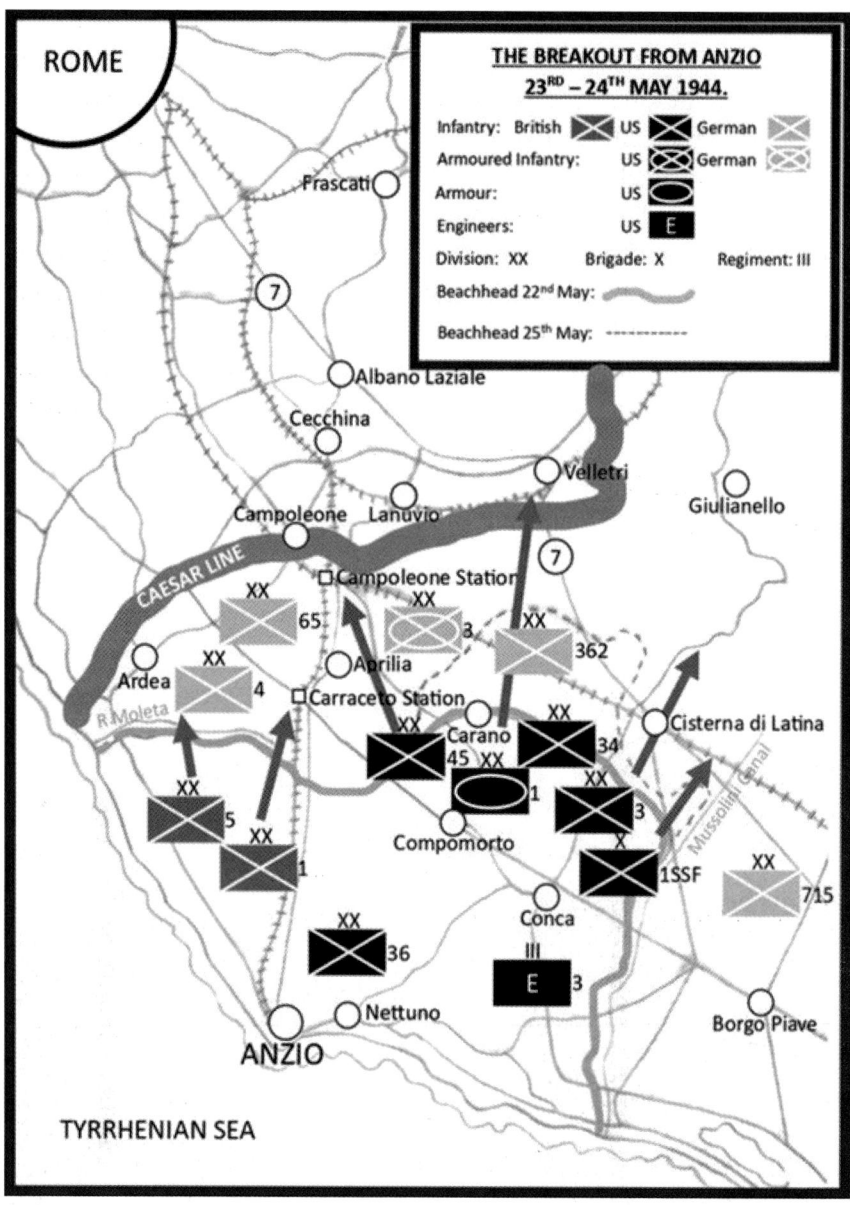

The headlights of all our lorries had shields on them but, even so, they were bright enough for the Jerries to have seen him running back with the PIAT, if they'd been looking in his direction, and they might've picked him off. As it was, they didn't, and the two of us set up the PIAT and fired from

─────── The Caesar Line, a Trip to Rome, and a Pig ───────

about 50 yards. Well, at that distance, it blew the bugger to blazes and it was still burning like a good 'un when we drove past it. I jumped out again and ran to snatch the aircraft recognition swastika off the back of it and nearly got toasted for my efforts. I've still got that flag, to tell the truth.

We pushed on, all the way to the Jerries' final defensive line, south of Rome. They called it the Caesar Line, and in the first week in June we took part in the attack on it, along with some American units. "A" Squadron had to attack a really important bridge on the main road into Rome, and "B" Squadron went to attack three ridges on their left. Support Squadron was divided between them, and I went with the attack on the bridge. A Jerry

45. PIAT in action, 1944. Loughlin (Sgt), No 2 Army Film & Photographic Unit. (Wikimedia Commons)

parachute battalion was trying to hold our bridge as well as the ridges, and they were bloody good, I can tell you, but we took them on, and we captured the bridge and the ridges, and 100 prisoners. The Yanks poured over our bridge and went tear-arsing up the road to Rome, while we got a visit from our divisional commander, Brigadier Loewen, who was in temporary charge because General Penny was in hospital after his car had been blown up. He congratulated us on what we'd done, which was nice of him.

Next day Rome fell, and at that point, me and Bricky decided to drive the 5 miles to the outskirts of the city, just for the hell of it. I didn't tell anyone I was doing it, because I didn't think they'd be that bothered; most of them were asleep, anyway. I reckoned that the Jerries must've all left, as near as dammit is to swearing, so I took the chance and joined an American column that was going north like the clappers.

We'd taken a jeep from the big vehicle park. Nobody'd paid any attention; there'd been all sorts of comings and goings as the British units straggled in from the south and the powers-that-be battled to bring some semblance of order to it all. I'd reckoned it would take a few days before the mess could be sorted out. They'd told us that the British weren't allowed into Rome… it was "Yanks only", but that only made us more determined, and we decided to push on into the city itself.

So, we took the Via del Mare, past this big church with a dome, and I had the idea of heading for the Vatican, to see if we could see the Pope, like. Everything was going hunky-dory until I took a wrong turn and ended up in a maze of side streets. I'd thought that the Vatican would be well signposted, but that would only have been on main streets, and I couldn't find any. I kept driving through a load of housing blocks, and as it was now late afternoon, I started to get a bit worried for the first time. There was no sign of life, nobody to ask for directions, and it definitely didn't look like the Rome I'd seen in magazines. Finally, we came to a road that was a bit wider, and I saw a sign for the "termini", which I guessed might be a bus station. It wasn't.

The main railway terminus in the city was a hive of activity as we pulled up in the square opposite. People were rushing about, most of them carrying suitcases, or packs on their backs, and none of them seemed to be celebrating their liberation, as I'd expected. Mind you, they all looked very peaky and underfed, so maybe they were just tired of all the war stuff. The kids were there, as usual, and we shared out all the chocolate we had.

46. Allied troops in Rome, June 1944. Tanner (Capt), War Office official photographer. (Wikimedia Commons)

A few teenage girls were standing round a lorry that had "American Red Cross" painted on the side. It had a sort of counter, and two soldiers with MP armbands and helmets were leaning on it, drinking what I supposed was coffee. They were grinning and laughing with the giggling lasses, and one seemed to be speaking the lingo.

My throat was as rough as the bottom of a birdcage, and I would've given my right arm for a mug of hot coffee, but there was no chance of us sidling across with an order…not while the police were standing there, like a pair of armed gorillas. They were bound to chuck us out on account of the "no Brits in the city" order. There was nowt for it but to keep sitting where we were until they decided to bugger off.

Two old ladies were sitting on the edge of the kerb nearby. They stared at us, and I kept trying to look away, but somehow, they drew me back with their unblinking, hollow eyes. I suppose that's what they were doing it for, but I still felt bad for them. They were dressed in black coits, with black hats that had probably been expensive once upon a time. They both had wrinkly stockings that drooped around sparrow-thin legs, and I reckoned they might have been twins. They carried on staring, and I took out my service book and pretended to read. Some scruffy looking bairns sidled up to us and, as usual, we handed them our chocolate ration and they scoffed the lot.

We'd been there a good half-hour when Bricky gave me a nudge. He nodded in the direction of the Red Cross lorry, and I turned to see the MPs strolling off, with the gang of girls at their heels. We tried to look all nonchalant as we hurried across the square and planted ourselves in front of the counter.

One of the lasses behind the serving hatch turned round to face us. The smile on her face disappeared for a second, as she gave us the once-over, but then she seemed to get a grip of herself as the smile returned and she asked what she could do for us. I kicked Bricky in the shin as he opened his mouth to answer her; knowing him as I did, I was certain that he was going to come out with summat vulgar.

"Two coffees, please," I said, as friendly as you like.

She turned to get the mugs and I took the opportunity to shake my head and glare at Bricky, as he rubbed his leg and stayed shtum.

"Didn't know there were any Tommies in town," said the girl, and she put two mugs of hot, steaming, black coffee in front of us.

"Got any milk?" said Bricky, and she handed over a tin jug.

"We got lost," I said.

"Where were you heading?"

"Vatican".

"Got an appointment, have you?" She obviously didn't believe me.

"What sandwiches you got?" said Bricky.

"Fried egg?" she said. "Real, not powdered".

What could we say? Hadn't had a real fried egg since we nicked some from an Arab in Africa and fried them on the side of a Bren gun carrier.

The fat was dribbling out of the bread cakes, as we turned and walked back to our bench, mug in one hand, sandwich in the other. The two old ladies were still there.

Bricky mumbled something as he sat down and took a huge bite of his sandwich.

"Fucking hell!" he said, and I got a face-full of grease and egg yolk. I told the bugger to watch it, but I knew what he meant. I tried to ignore them, and I did ok for two bites, then I gave up.

"Oh, bugger it!"

I gave what was left of the sandwich to one of the ladies. She grabbed it without a word, before tearing it in two and handing half to her chum. Both of them stuffed their mouths and chewed away like Billy-O, as the fat ran down their old chins, bless 'em! For once, Bricky did the reight thing and handed over his sandwich. He got a gracious nod for his pains, before the grub disappeared into their cakeholes.

After we'd shared the coffee, we sat back and watched the only cloud in the sky, as it drifted south. A sign of weather to come, I remember thinking at the time. I told you that I allus seem to remember the daftest things, didn't I?

Anyroad, Bricky nudged me again, and I turned to see the two MPs walk back into the square. They looked like they were setting off on a patrol of the area.

"What we going to do?" says Bricky.

In truth, I hadn't a clue, but my old lady seemed to take in the situation with one look. She grabbed my arm and beckoned me towards what looked like a black hole. As I didn't have an idea of my own, I did as she bid me, and we all shuffled into the cool dark of a smelly alleyway.

A cat screeched as we disturbed its sleep, and an empty bottle flew out of a high window to smash against the wall and shower us with glass.

"Where we goin?" asked Bricky. "This looks pretty dodgy to me."

He was right. I reckoned we were in one of Rome's seedy areas, but I didn't have a better idea, so I let the woman drag me further into the maze of alleys.

Finally, we came out onto what looked like a little square where several alleys all met. As we did, my woman seemed to fall sideways, and I was knocked over by a pig. I kid you not… it was a pig! Well, half a pig. It was over the shoulder of a dodgy-looking little bloke, who went arse-over-tit across the square and landed in a heap, against some dustbins. The side of pork landed on top of him. He staggered to his feet, dripping summat nasty that must have been in the bins, and panted like a set of bellows as he struggled to pull out a gun from his sock. I drew my service revolver and it seemed to calm him down a bit.

The little old lady obviously knew him, as she wrapped herself round his shoulder and started jabbering in his earhole. She kept looking in my direction, and each time his eyes followed hers, before turning back to her as his own blathering joined in the noise. Finally, he shrugged her off and stamped his foot as he yelled summat.

"Shit!" said Bricky.

At that point, somebody pushed me in the back that hard I fell on my knees, and I heard a voice say,

"What the fuck is going on here?"

One of the American MP's was standing over me, revolver in hand. Quick as a flash, he pointed it at the pig man. They stared at each other for quite a bit, before the second MP stepped into the light and pointed his gun at the Eyetie.

"Drop it!" he shouts.

"Bloody hell! Just like the cowboys!" says Bricky, too loud for my liking.

The first MP said summat in Italian. I reckoned he was giving the Eyetie a Scarborough warning because the man shrugged and pushed his gun inside his jacket. I noticed that the Americans kept their weapons up.

After that, they all got together and started chin-wagging in Italian. The little old ladies got involved, and the Yanks put their guns back in their holsters, while me and Bricky went and sat on the bins to light up our fags and watch the commotion.

After a bit, one of the Yanks came over to us, all friendly-like. He said that they'd seen us in the square and were coming over to have a chat with us, when we got up and trundled off down the alley. He said he'd heard all about

The Caesar Line, a Trip to Rome, and a Pig

General Clark's order to keep Rome as an American-only zone, but that he, personally, thought it was a load of horse shit. I remember that clearly.

"A load of horse shit."

I'd never heard that before, and I filed it away in the store of insults I kept in my head, for emergencies.

It seemed that the Eyetie had nicked the pig from a Yank supply truck and was planning to roast it and sell it on the black market. The Yank had told him that he couldn't possibly allow American property to be sold on by the "fucking mafia," (I filed that one away anall) and he'd said that, by all accounts, he should arrest the bloke and take the pig back to its rightful owners. Then he'd had a bit of a think about it. Who could tell, he said, who the rightful owners were? The supply people had probably nicked it from some poor, Eyetie farmer, and they were probably intending to scoff the pig themselves. He'd had experience with these supply people before; rob their own mothers, he said they would. Then there was all the paperwork involved in arresting an Eyetie and two Limeys,

"Think of the political trouble it could cause," he said.

No, he thought, much too much trouble involved. On the other hand, he'd had a better idea altogether. He'd arranged with the pig man to drop all charges on the understanding that they would all share the pig amongst themselves.

Bricky asked if we would be included and the Yank clapped him around the shoulders and said summat about friends and allies, all in it together. I reckon he meant that we should keep our traps shut, and so we readily agreed to the plan.

So, we ended up in a dingy bar that was only lit by candles stuck to the greasy tables that stank of sour wine and puke. The pig man, whose name was Lorenzo, told the bloke behind the bar, who was called Tommaso, to dump the side of pig in the yard, and went out back to bring out a fat, dark-skinned woman. He seemed to be introducing her, and I heard the name Lucia.

Lucia set about pulling down a load of bottles from a shelf behind the bar. It was all wine, and I'd never drunk much of the stuff, but by now I was gagging. As Lorenzo tossed his hat onto a bust of Mussolini that seemed to have been nailed to the wall, Lucia and Tommaso went into the yard and started to drag the pig towards what looked like a spit thing. It seemed that pig-roasting was not summat new around here. They fetched some wood from an outhouse and started a fire.

47. The author, with the Nazi flag that his father took from a German tank at Anzio, 1944. (Roger Holgate)

Bricky asked how long it would take, and the Yank asked Lorenzo.

"Five hours", he said. "Plenty time! Plenty time!"

He stuck a full wine glass in my hand.

"Saluti! Saluti! Saluti! Saluti! All friends! Fuck Il Duce!"

Everyone joined in the toast

"Pax Romana!" I said. Don't know where that came from, but everybody seemed impressed.

547113 SQMS H. Holgate
HQ Sqn 9th KOYLI
QOYD
CMF
21-6-44

Dear Kit.

Many thanks for your letter which I received today, and also for the very many others which I haven't answered. You certainly felt in the mood for writing according to what you managed to get on this letter card. You begin by saying that Edith and Carroll had been up to your house after they had been into town to buy Mary her birthday present, and that reminds me to try and get her something from Rome when I go again, which I hope will be tomorrow. I went on Sunday, but the shops were all closed. I think that silk stockings and handbags are cheap there, so maybe they are what I shall acquire if possible. Poor old lass, I bet she thinks I am a good guy, forgetting my wife's birthday, but I shall rectify that just as soon as the opportunity arises. What is the big idea, Kit, getting in touch with Mrs W A regarding my health**. I don't think they can do much, even by getting in touch with someone at this end. The answer she will receive will be "he's OK" because I have already told them when I got back that I was alright. No Kit, I have still got the trouble yet although it isn't so bad. What I want to do is wait until I get home, then go sick and get the proper treatment: that is dieting for about six months which can't be done out here because they haven't got the time and stuff to do it with. So, Mary is cracking up with overworking, is she? Well, tell her that she has to either give up her work, or let the house clean itself. Again, remind her that it isn't a thing to get excited over yet as I don't suppose we shall be home for quite a spell yet. Anyway, even if I was coming home tomorrow, I wouldn't give a hang about the house, just as long as there were a couple of orange boxes to sit on and a roof. The only thing I look forward to is seeing her and the kids looking well and fit, so will you tell her that I have found out that she is over doing things. As for getting all the money together that she can for after the war, she has to pack up if it means her health is being jeopardized. I can send her what she wants if she only tells me, as I don't spend a great deal these days. By the time you get this she should have received another £25, which I think will put her over the 100 mark. Of course, I wouldn't have been able to spend it had I been on a job other than the fighting line. You want to know what I think of the invasion? Well, to tell you the truth the only comment I have is that it only just started in time. I do think that Jerry will be about ready to pack up by Xmas, everywhere he is having his setbacks. I am not worried about being in at the kill; I guess I have had enough. What do you think? I don't know what the idea of Grigg's*** is, but keeping us out here for five years, it's too much of a gap in a married couple's life, war or no war. You can't tell me there isn't enough manpower to relieve what few are out here with that four years' service abroad. Why couldn't we have been sent home a few months ago, for a change, then put us in the second front, the fighting there can't be any worse than what we have experienced at Alamein and Anzio. Another way to look at it is that the lads who are now prisoners and those who have been killed here, would have been able to see their loved ones, and most of them would, no doubt, have been alive today.

So, old Pat was giving you a bit of back chat, was she? And her reply to what you said was "well. My Daddy likes me as I am!" Of course I do! Bless them all! Out here, it makes my heart bleed to see the kiddies. They simply mob you if you show them a bar of chocolate, or a sandwich. I told you that I had been for a day's outing to Rome; well, I sat on a bench under some trees to eat my sandwich, and near us were two real old ladies. As soon as I began to eat, they both turned and really goggled at me. Well, I ask you, could you have gone on eating with two old ladies like that, almost jumping over the seat? No, and neither could I. If you could have seen the way they shared that sandwich and about gulped it down, it would have made you wonder. And everyone is the same. I had a bar of chocolate and about twenty kiddies round. Well, what could I do with a bar? I shared it out to six and pinched my mate's out of the haversack and shared that, and the remainder of the kids that didn't get any looked on, wondering if some other soldier would come up and give them a bit.

Well. I guess this will have to do this time. I could have written more on Italy and its people but space won't allow, so I will say goodnight and God bless you all at home.

Best love xx
Harry

J xx C xx Pxx M xx Edith xx Mary xxxxxxx
** Author's Note: "Mrs WA" refers to Joyce, wife of Lieutenant-Colonel J.R.P. Warde-Aldam, High Sheriff of Yorkshire who took command of the Queen's Own Yorkshire Dragoons in 1939, and who knew Harry, personally. For several years after the war, Harry received a brace of pheasants as a Christmas gift from the Warde-Aldams.

*** Author's Note: Sir James Grigg, Churchill's Secretary of State for War, had suggested that any soldier who had served overseas for more than four years should be called home to complete their war service in Britain, and not be required to serve in mainland Europe.

48. Party for the families of serving Dragoons, Danum Ballroom, Doncaster, January 1944. Mrs Warde-Aldam is 4th from left, back row. Harry's family are seated in front of the table on the right. (The Doncaster Chronicle)

SESSION 22

Florence, Morpeth, and Home

We got back to our lads a couple of days later and, as I'd guessed, nobody seemed to have noticed we'd gone.

We got told that, after the business on the Caesar Line, our regiment had got a cartload of medals. We lost over 300 blokes in that one attack, killed, wounded, or missing, and I was just glad to be alive, I can tell you.

We were transferred back to 1st Armoured Division, who had apparently missed us, before they moved us up to Florence for a bit, and we went back into the line on the outskirts of the city. Then they said we were going to a place called Porto Recanati on the Adriatic, where 1st Armoured were going back into the attack on the next line that Jerry had set up. I asked myself if they were ever going to run out of lines. They called this one The Gothic Line, and I wondered if they'd run out of stupid, bloody names, before they ran out of lines.

Then, at the end of August, we were told that all of us original Yorkshire Dragoons, who'd been in it for four and a half years, were going home: there were 300 of us left. I don't know what I felt really; numb, I suppose. It was one of those life changing moments, like leaving school, getting married, having a family and such, that leave your head spinning and your world turned upside down. I stayed like that all the way back to Naples, when I had a shower in one of the tents set up by the RASC, the best meal I'd had for months, and a good night's sleep. When you're up to your neck in muck and bullets, the one thing you want more than anything else, including grub, is sleep, and I was jiggered. I got new, clean battledress, and shirts and socks and boots, all in a neatly folded bundle like the one they'd given me all those years ago, in Canterbury. We sailed on 31st August, three days before the rest of the regiment attacked The Gothic Line. I felt sorry for them, and a bit guilty, to tell the truth, but I'd had enough, and I think I slept most of the way home.

49. Doncaster Railway Station, September 1944. Left to Right: Julie, Kit, Mary, Pat, Harry, and Carroll. (© Roger Holgate)

I ended up in Berwick-upon-Tweed for a bit, then got moved to Morpeth near Newcastle, where I had a letter from your mum. Aunt Sally and Uncle Lige lived in Morpeth, so she could come and stay with them, she said, and see me while she was at it. When she came, she gave me the bottle of Barnsley Bitter that the landlord of The Tavern had given her as a sort of welcome home, like. I can't remember much about our meeting, except for the Barnsley Bitter. I was still numb, I suppose.

After a few weeks, the camp was starting to give me the willies, and it was a relief to be told that I could go home. As the train pulled into Donny station, I said goodbye to the Goole lads who'd been with me from the start. Then I stepped onto the platform and my two girls ran to meet me. I don't think they'd have recognized me, but your mum must've pointed me out to them and so they came running. Auntie Kit and Julie were there too, and we all went home.

Appendix I

On 22nd November 1944, Lt. General R.L. McCreery, Commander of the British Eighth Army, sent the following message to all ranks, Queen's Own Yorkshire Dragoons:

"The Commander in Chief has written to your commanding officer telling him of his great regret that your splendid unit has got to be placed in suspended animation, and that the shortage of manpower is the reason for this decision being taken. I want to endorse all that the Commander in Chief has said, and to add to it my own personal regret that the traditions and loyalties that have grown up in five years of war service must now be dissolved.

Your regiment has a distinguished record in this war. You have undertaken many tasks and done them all well. In Syria and the Western Desert, you were in action, and at El Alamein in your new role as a motor battalion in 2nd Armoured Brigade you fought with great gallantry and determination. You were again in action in the decisive battle to break the Mareth Line, and in the final stage of the African campaign when 1st Armoured Division took part in the breakthrough which led to the capture of Tunis.

In Italy, you had your full share of the fierce defensive fighting in the Anzio bridgehead, followed by a successful advance to the River Tiber. Finally, you fought with a fine endurance and determination to break The Gothic Line defences on the Coriano Ridge. This is a splendid fighting record and one of which you can all be justly proud.

Times have changed since the early days of the war, and final victory is certain. But it is not yet achieved. Victory can be hastened

Appendix I

only by the greatest exertions on the part of us all, and I know I can rely on ALL ranks to fight as hard and as well in the future to finish the job off quickly as they have in the past with the Queen's Own Yorkshire Dragoons.

R.L. McCreery,
Lieut. General,
Commander,
Eighth Army."

Appendix II

General H.R. Alexander, sent the following communication to Lt. Colonel A.J.S. Tarrant, Commanding Officer, Queen's Own Yorkshire Dragoons, from Headquarters, Allied Armies in Italy, CMF:

"My Dear Tarrant,

It is my great regret that your distinguished regiment has to be placed in suspended animation. As an old regimental officer myself, I well recognize the disappointment it will cause amongst your grand chaps who have done so awfully well in Italy. You have a very fine old record and have had a marked variety of activities on the battlefield during the last forty years. I hate to see fine old units disbanded or put on the shelf, but you realize that the whole trouble is lack of men to keep units up to strength.

You may well be proud of the part your regiment has played in our great victories out here, and I shall always feel very proud to have had the Yorkshire Dragoons under my command.

Yours sincerely,
H.R. Alexander."

Appendix III

Above and overleaf: Army Form of Attestation. Harry Holgate 17th February 1927. (© Roger Holgate)

CERTIFIED COPY OF ATTESTATION

No. .... Name HOLGATE Harry Corps of Hussars of the Line

§Regiment Selected .... ‡(To be entered in case of Cavalry.)

Questions to be put to the Recruit before Enlistment

1. What is your Full Name? — 1. Christian Name ... Harry / Surname ... Holgate
2. In or near what Parish or Town were you born? — 2. In the Parish of .... in or near the Town of .... in the County of York
3. (a) Are you a British Subject? / (b) Nationality of Parents at their birth? — 3. (a) .... (b) Father English Mother ...
4. What is the date of your birth and age? — 4. 29-?-1904 Age 18 Yrs ... Days
5. What is your Trade or Calling? — 5. ...
6. (a) Are you Married? (b) How many children are dependent upon you? — 6. (a) No (b) No
7. [Militia/Reserve question] — 7. No
8. Have you ever served in the Royal Navy, the Army, Royal Air Force... — 8. No
9. Have you truly stated the whole, if any, of your previous service? — 9. Yes
10. Are you, or have you been, an Apprentice? — 10. No
11. Have you ever been sentenced to penal servitude or imprisonment by the civil power? — 11. No
12. Have you ever been rejected as unfit for the Naval, Military or Air Forces of the Crown? — 12. No
13. Are you willing to be vaccinated or re-vaccinated? — 13. Yes
14. For what Corps are you willing to be enlisted...? — 14. Corps of Hussars of the Line
15. If you are enlisting for service in the Cavalry... — 15. RB
16. Do you understand that, notwithstanding you enlist for a dismounted Corps, you are liable to be trained and employed in such mounted duties as may be... — 16. RB

17. Are you willing to serve upon the following conditions provided His Majesty should so long require your services? — 17. Yes

18. Are you willing to serve upon the following conditions provided His Majesty should so long require your services? — 18. RB

19. Have you received a notice paper stating the liabilities you are incurring by enlisting... — 19. Yes — Name ... Marshall

I, Harry Holgate, do solemnly declare that the above answers made by me to the above questions are true, and that I am willing to fulfil the engagements made; also that I understand that, should my health fail or should I sustain an injury during service in the Army, I shall not be eligible for consideration for pension or gratuity on account of disability unless the disability is attributable to the conditions of Military Service.

A. Kenton PPC — Signature of Witness. Harry Holgate — Signature of Recruit.

OATH TO BE TAKEN BY RECRUIT ON ATTESTATION

I, Harry Holgate, swear by Almighty God, that I will be faithful and bear true Allegiance to His Majesty King George the Fifth, His Heirs, and Successors, and that I will, as in duty bound, honestly and faithfully defend His Majesty, His Heirs, and Successors, in Person, Crown, and Dignity against all enemies, and will observe and obey all orders of His Majesty, His Heirs, and Successors, and of the Generals and Officers set over me. So help me God.

CERTIFICATE OF MAGISTRATE OR ATTESTING OFFICER

The Recruit above-named was cautioned by me that if he made any false answer to any of the above questions he would be liable to be punished as provided in the Army Act.

The above questions were then read to the Recruit in my presence.

I have taken care that he understands each question, and that his answer to each question has been duly entered as replied to, and the said recruit has made and signed the declaration and taken the oath before me at .... on this 29.1.1927 .... day.

Signature of the Justice ...

If any alteration is required on this page of the Attestation, a Justice of the Peace should be requested to make it and initial the alteration under Section 80 (6), Army Act. The Recruit should receive a copy of his attestation on Army Form B. 271A.

NOTE — ...ter must erase Question 17 or 18 and complete the remaining Questions before handing the form to the Recruit.

Appendix IV

Serial No. 646 15 KRH.
Army Form B.108.

Regular Army

Certificate of Service.

Army No. 547113
Surname HOLGATE
Christian Names Harry
Enlisted at Leeds
Enlisted on 17th February 1927
Corps for which enlisted Hussars of the Line

NOTE.—Attention is specially directed to Pages 2, 6 & 7.

Above and overleaf spread: Certificate of Service. Harry Holgate. 26th February 1933. (© Roger Holgate)

2   (This page should be entirely free from erasure.)

Final Assessments of Conduct and Character on Leaving the Colours.

Military Conduct *Exemplary.*

Testimonial
A very reliable man, clean, honest and sober. He has been employed as forage orderly, in which position he has given very satisfaction.

The above assessments have been read to the soldier.

Signature of Soldier on Transfer to Reserve or on Discharge   H Holgate L/c
(Delete words which are inapplicable.)

Place Risalpur.

Date 26·2·33.

J H Mace Signature and Rank Lieut-Colonel
O.C., 15th The King's Royal Hussars.

Appendix IV

Service with the Colours showing Transfers, if any, to other Corps.

Corps	Country	From	To	Length of Service	
				Years	Days
Hussars of the Line	Home	14-2-27	30-7-27		168
Cavalry of the Line	Home	31-7-27	30-12-29	2	153
"	India	31-12-29	29-3-33	3	89
	Home	30-3-33	14-4-33	–	16

3

Appendix V

Certificate of Transfer to the Army Reserve. Harry Holgate. 4th April 1933. (© Roger Holgate)

Appendix VI

Certificate of Discharge.

Date of discharge... 16th February 1939
Rank... Trooper
Cause of discharge... Termination of first period of Engagement – Para: 1510 (Vii) KR
Corps from which discharged... Cavalry of the Line (15/9th)

Service on date of discharge :–
(a) With Colours... Six years – 57 days.
(b) In the Reserve... Five years 308 days.
TOTAL SERVICE... Twelve years NIL days.

Description of soldier on discharge* :–
Year of birth... Height... ft... ins.
Complexion... Eyes... Hair...
Marks or Scars...

Signature and rank: R. Hubbard, Captain
Place: Canterbury
Date: 14-2-39
Officer i/c Cavalry Records.

* Not required to be completed in the case of a man discharged from the Army Reserve.

Certificate of Discharge. Harry Holgate. 14th February 1939. (© Roger Holgate)

Appendix VII

Educational Attainments, Trade Qualifications, Medals. Harry Holgate. 14th February 1939. (© Roger Holgate)

Appendix VIII

Army Book 64 (Part I).

Soldier's Service Book.

(Soldier's Pay Book, Army Book 64 (Part II), will be issued for active service.)

Entries in this book (other than those connected with the making of a Soldier's Will and insertion of the names of relatives) are to be made under the superintendence of an Officer.

Instructions to Soldier.

1. You are held **personally responsible** for the safe custody of this book.
2. You will **always carry this book** on your person.
3. You must produce the book whenever called upon to do so by a competent military authority, viz., Officer, Warrant Officer, N.C.O. or Military Policeman.
4. You must not alter or make any entry in this book (except as regards your next-of-kin on pages 10 and 11 or your Will on pages 15 to 20).
5. Should you lose the book, you will report the matter to your immediate military superior.
6. On your transfer to the Army Reserve this book will be handed into your Orderly Room for transmission, through the O. i/c Records, to place of rejoining on mobilization.
7. You will be permitted to retain this book after discharge, but should you lose the book after discharge it will not be replaced.
8. If you are discharged from the Army Reserve, this book will be forwarded to you by the O. i/c Records.

Pages 165–172: Soldier's Service Book. Harry Holgate. 27th October 1944. (© Roger Holgate)

2

(1) SOLDIER'S NAME and DESCRIPTION on ATTESTATION.

Army Number **54 7113**
Surname (in capitals) .... **HOLGATE**
Christian Names (in full) .... **HARRY**
Date of Birth **29/7/08**
Place of Birth.
 - Parish .... ▓▓▓
 - In or near the town of .... ▓▓▓
 - In the county of .... ▓▓▓
Trade on Enlistment .... *Rlwy Shunter*

Nationality of Father at birth .... ▓▓▓
Nationality of Mother at birth .... ▓▓▓
Religious Denomination .... *C of E*
Approved Society .... *Prudential Ins. Coy.*
Membership No. ....
Enlisted at .... *Doncaster* .... On *21/4/39*

For the:—
 * Regular Army.   * Supplementary Reserve.
 * Territorial Army.   * Army Reserve Section D.
      * Strike out those inapplicable.

For .... years with the Colours and .... years in the Reserve.

Particulars of former
service Army No.,
Corps or Regiment
and period.
 .... *6 yrs Colours*
 .... *4 " Reserve*

Signature of Soldier .... *H Holgate*
Date .... **21 . 10 . 44 .**

Appendix VIII

3

DESCRIPTION ON ENLISTMENT.

Height ....5........ft. ...8 ¾....ins.   Weight ...10...:..0..lbs.

Maximum Chest ....36......ins.   Complexion...Fresh....

Eyes ....Hazel............   Hair......Fair......

Distinctive Marks and Minor Defects ....

........Scars NIL........

....

......R.A.S.C. 15(c)........

......6/3/4/241......G.D.K. Cholmondeley Major

....

CONDITION ON TRANSFER TO RESERVE.

Found fit for ....

Defects or History of past illness which should be enquired into if called up for Service ....

....

....

....

Date..................19.........

Initials of M.O, i/c...

A 2

4
PARTICULARS OF TRAINING.

Courses and Schools. Specialist Qualifications. Showing result.	Date.	Initials of Officer.
Gas Chamber Test	April 1941	
" "	3-2-42	
Promoted A/U/Sgt P.T.O N°2 (13-1-41)	31-12-40	
Appointed A/P/Sgt WEF 3-2-41 PTO5	21-1-41	
Middle East School of Artillery Gnr Course	31-8-42	
APPOINTED P/A/SQMS. PTO N°58	13-9-42	
W.S. C.Q.M.S. PTO. 13.	15-9-42	
	13-3-44	
Awarded Africa Star with 8th Army Clasp P.T.O. No. 4 4/2/44	7.6.44	
Gas Chamber Test (CAP)	1 Nov 44	
Attended Clerks Course No 2 at No 2 T.T.Gp (Tech College Smethwick) classified as Learner Clerk(D) W.E.F.	14 June 45	

Appendix VIII

RECORD OF SPECIALIST EMPLOYMENT WHILST SERVING.*

Period.		Nature of Employment.	Remarks and Initials of Officer.
From	To		
		Record of Leave	Free Warrant
2.2.44	7.10.44	28 Days Disem. Leave	Yes.
15/2/45	11.4.45	10 Days P.d. Leave	Yes.
22.2.45	6.6.45	9 Days P.d. Leave	Yes.
PD 14.6.45 to 16:00 hrs 25.6.45. 11 Days Pass			YES
3/8/45 to 12/8/45		9 day Pur + VE	YES

*To include (1) as Skilled Tradesman, (2) as Specialist, e.g., Signaller or M. Gunner.

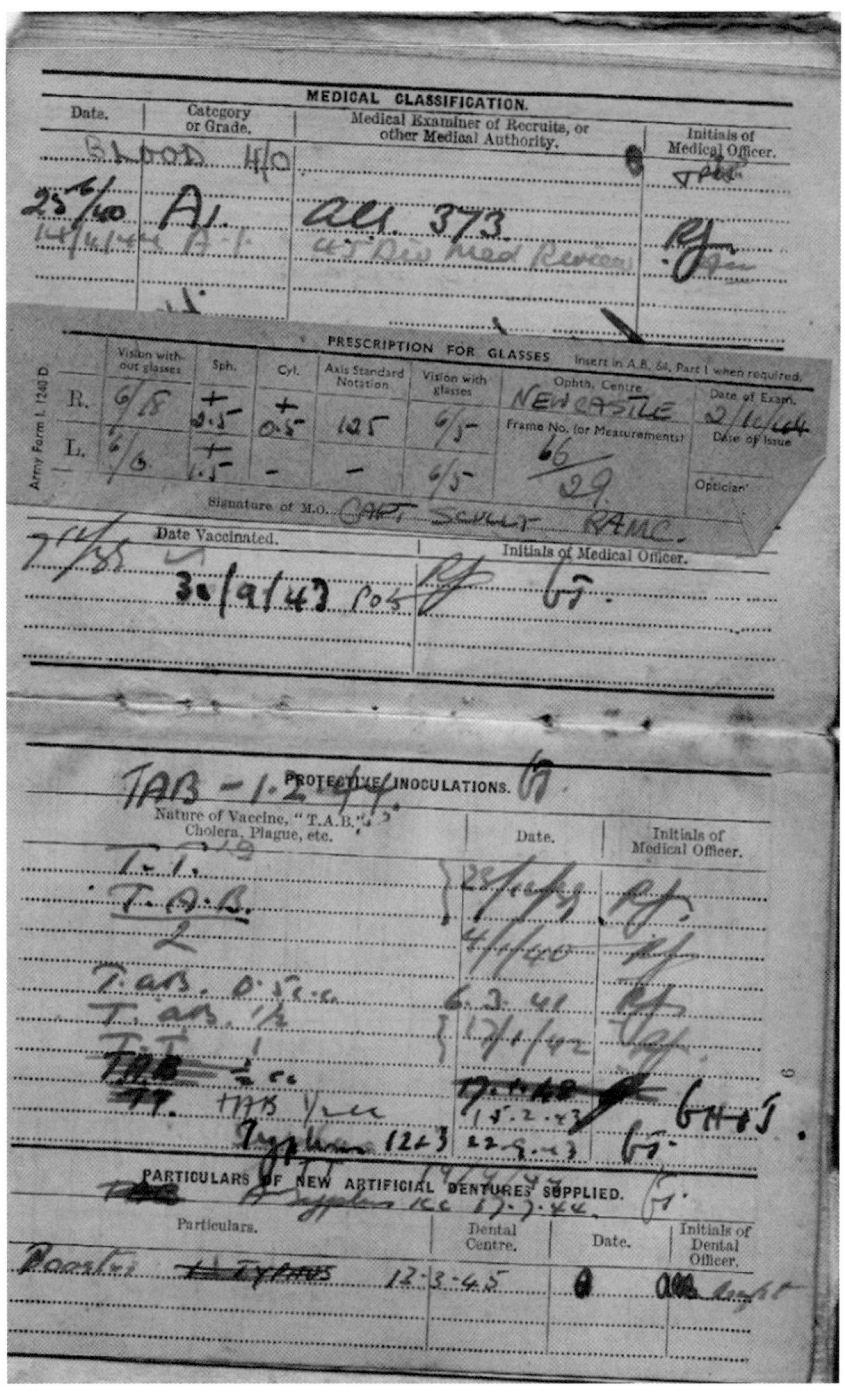

Appendix VIII

NEXT OF KIN

Any change becoming known is to be duly noted with date of
NOTE.—No entry in these pages has any legal effect as a WILL (see

Nearest degree of relationship.	Names.	Date.
Wife.	Mrs. Holgate M.E	
Children.	Carroll Holgate Elaine Patricia Holgate	
Father.		
Mother.		
* Brothers and Sisters.		
Other Relations (stating relationship)		

* State whether brothers are older or younger.

NOW LIVING.

such change and reported by O.C. Unit to the Officer i/c Records. pages 12 to 14).

Latest known Address in full.

28 Dudley Rd Intake
Doncaster Yorkshire
England

Appendix IX

TRANSCRIPT

YORKSHIRE DRAGOONS in SYRIA.

Saw End of Vichy Regime.

Yorkshire Dragoons—many of them hailing from Doncaster—took part in the military ceremonial when Syria was occupied by British and French troops and the Vichy regime came to an end. Their arrival in the country of the Druses is thus described:

"The French troops were entitled to all the honours of war, so, passing through the cantonment, General Dunn led his Yorkshire Dragoons to the garrison racecourse. Here, upon high ground commanding a vast expanse of hill and plain, its harsh contours mellowed by the haze of heat and dust, the Dragoons paraded as a guard of honour to the three companies of the departing French. Bronzed under their sun helmets, armed with flashing sabres, and well mounted, the Dragoons made a brave and efficient array.

Newspaper article: 28th July 1941. (Doncaster Chronicle. Public domain)

"The French infantry looked rather worse for wear and were weighed down by heavy packs, but they stepped out jauntily as, with flags flying and the band playing, Commandant Bouvet marched them past the guard of honour. Druse gendarmerie upon Arab chargers then led the garrison of 1,800 officers and men out of the town and the Union Jack replaced the Tricolour upon the tower of the fort.

"The brigade afterwards marched past Brigadier Dunn. The Dragoons led off followed by the infantry attached to the brigade—a battalion of the Essex Regiment which distinguished itself at Palmyra. In the light uniform and equipment, marching in column of threes with bayonets fixed, they moved upon the rough ground with precision. There was also an Australian anti-tank detachment, a troop of mechanized field artillery, and an endless procession of ambulances and transport vehicles. Low overhead roared British bombers. The Druses had seen for the first time, and upon impressive scale, a demonstration of British strength, order, and discipline."

Appendix X

Record of Service. Harry Holgate. 10th October 1945. (© Roger Holgate)

Appendix XI

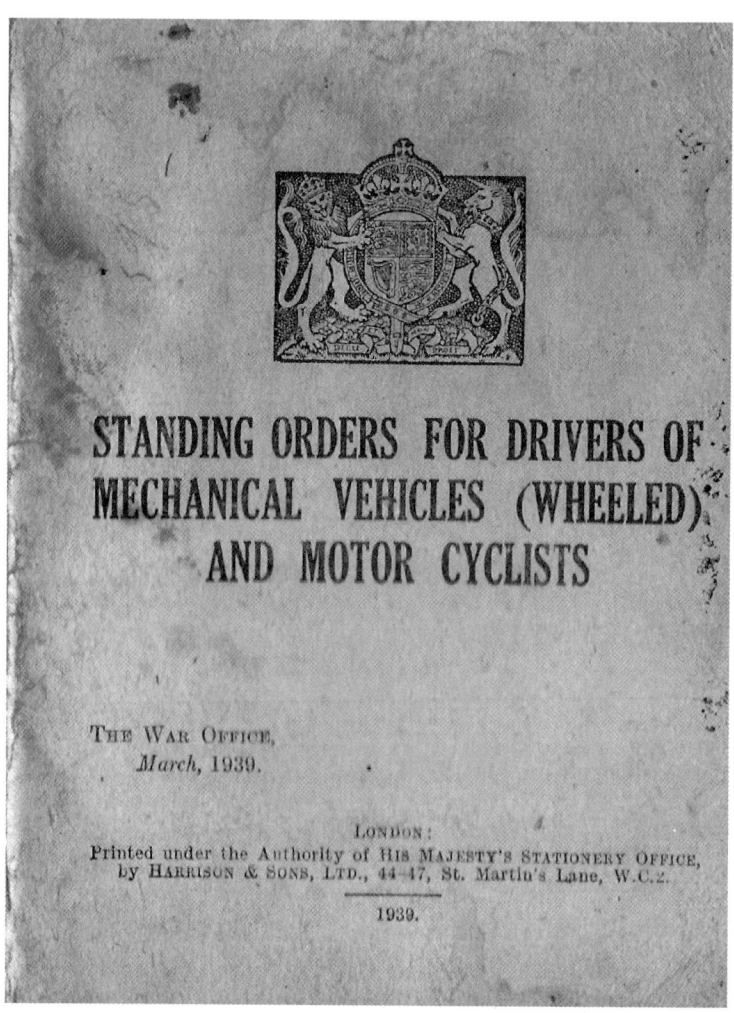

Standing Orders for Drivers. March 1939. (© Roger Holgate)

Appendix XII

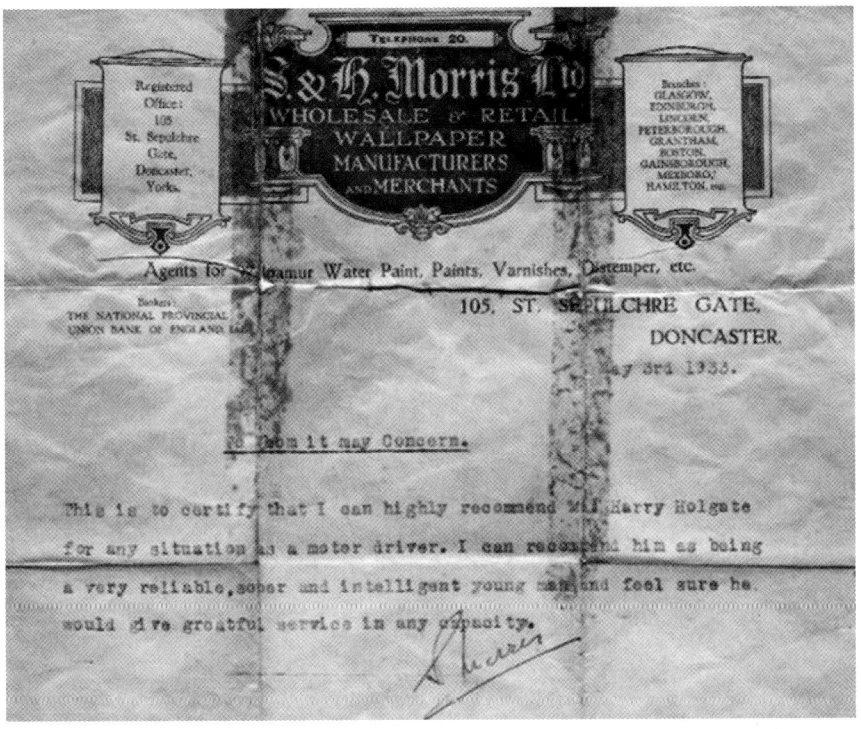

Character Reference from Sammy Morris. May 1933. (© Roger Holgate)

TRANSCRIPT

To whom it may concern: This is to certify that I can highly recommend Mr Harry Holgate for any situation as a motor driver. I can recommend him as being a very reliable, sober, and intelligent young man and feel sure he would give grateful service in any capacity.

S. Morris

Appendix XIII

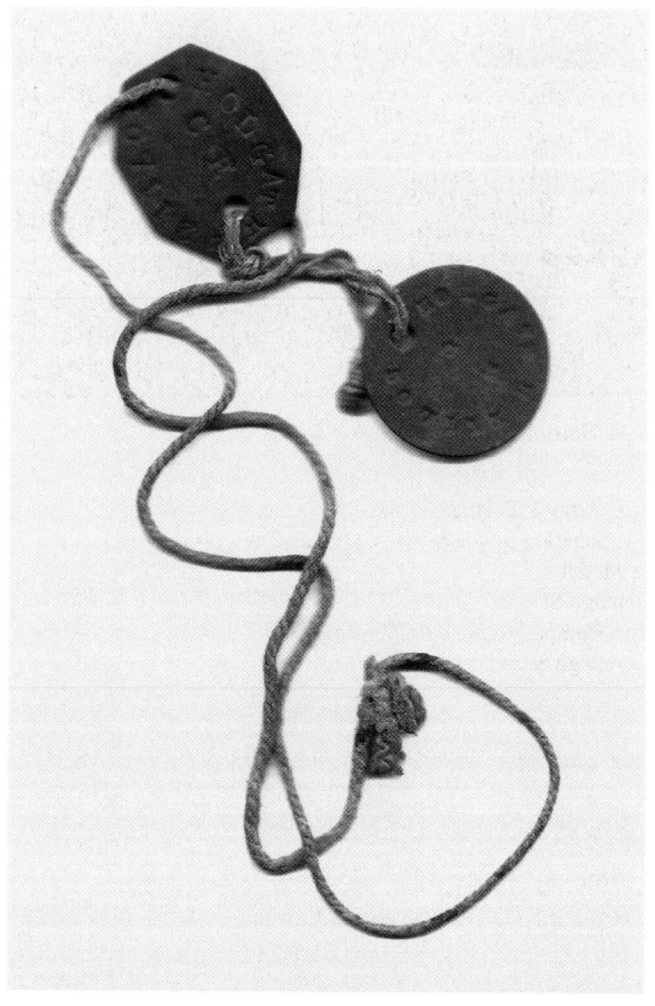

W.W.2 Identification Tags. Harry Holgate. (© Roger Holgate)

Appendix XIV

Service Medals. Harry Holgate. (© Roger Holgate)

Left to right:
1939 Territorial Army Efficiency Medal
1930–31 India General Service Medal with North-West Frontier clasp
1939–45 War Medal
1939 45 Campaign Star
1940–43 Africa Campaign Star with 8th Army clasp
1944 Italy Campaign Star

Appendix XV

Dried flowers postcard to Julie, sent from Uncle Addy, Jerusalem, November 1942.

Glossary

Addled	Confused.
Allus	Always.
Alreight	Alright.
Anall	Also.
Antwacky	Antique.
Anyroad	Anyway.
Apeth	Fool. From an old Yorkshire term for a halfpenny which, being worth little, was considered silly, or useless.
Arse	A person's buttocks, or anus.
Arse-over-tit	Used when someone has fallen hard. *He fell arse-over-tit down the stairs.*
At a pinch	*With a bit of luck.*
Bad job	Wrong. Unjust. Distasteful.
Backards	Backwards.
Bagamashings	A jumbled mess.
Bairns	Children.
Barmy	Stupid.
Barmpot	A silly person.
Barnsley Bitter	A popular, South Yorkshire beer.

Before you could say Jack Robinson	A phrase used to indicate that something happened very quickly.
Bent as a nine-bob note	Extremely dishonest and criminally minded.
Bint	Derogatory term for a woman. From the Arab word "bint," meaning girl or daughter.
Black-bright	Very dirty.
Blighty	England.
Brickin' mesen	"I'm very frightened."
Bobby-dazzler	Outstanding, striking, or showy.
Bob's your uncle	Phrase used to mean very simple. Without fuss.
Bollocking	An admonishment.
Bog	Toilet.
Boggart	A ghost, or spectre.
Braying	Beating violently.
Brew	A cup of tea.
Bugger	A term of mild abuse for a man. *"You silly bugger!"*
Bugger-all	Nothing.
Butties	Sandwiches.
Cadged	Asked for, or obtained, usually by begging.
Cack-handed	Clumsy.
Came up trumps	Carried out an activity that led to success.
Cantonment	A military garrison, or camp.
Carried a torch for	Felt attracted to.
Carting	Carrying.

Glossary

Chelp	Rude, or cheeky remarks.
Chuck-up	To vomit.
Chuffy	Arrogant, disdainful.
Chuntering	Grumbling.
Chinwag	Casual conversation.
Clacker	The uvula.
Clagged-up	Blocked, congested.
Clap cold	Freezing.
Cock-up	Something done badly, or inefficiently.
Coits	Coats.
Daft	Silly, stupid.
Decked	Knocked to the floor.
Didn't know if I was on this earth, or Fuller's	Totally perplexed. Fuller's earth is a type of absorbent clay.
Dum-dum bullet	A bullet that has been filed so that it causes maximum damage.
Dunno	"I don't know."
Earwigging	Secretly listening to a conversation.
'Eck	Used for emphasis in questions and exclamations. *"What the 'eck's the matter?"*
EPIP	European Personnel Indian Pattern (tent).
Eyeties	British army derogatory term for "Italians."
Faffing	Spending time in ineffectual activity.
Fair parky	Very cold.
Fer	For.
Fettled	Clean and scrubbed.

Flummoxed	Bewildered. Perplexed.
Forrards	Forwards.
Fred Carno's Circus	A phrase used to describe a scene of chaos.
Fritten	Frighten.
Gansey	A jacket.
Gawping	Staring fixedly, and open-mouthed.
Gen	Information.
Ginnel	Alleyway.
Give 'em what for	To punish, or rebuke.
Gob	Mouth.
Gobfull	A lot of verbal abuse.
Gobsmacked	Astounded, amazed.
Gobshite	Someone who engages in irritating, or offensive language.
Got the monk on	Irritated, annoyed.
Grub	Food.
Guidon	Regimental flag.
Gumption	Determination and courage.
Half-inch	To steal.
Happy as Larry	Extremely happy.
Hell for leather	Very fast.
Innit?	Isn't it?
It's a tale	It isn't going to happen.
Jacksie	A person's buttocks, or anus.
Jammy	Extremely fortunate.
Jerry	British army slang for "Germans."

Glossary

Jerry can	A pressed steel fuel container, originally designed in Germany.
Jiggered	Tired, exhausted.
Jittery	Nervous.
Jockstrap	A support for male genitals, worn especially by sportsmen.
Knocked into the middle of next week	Severely dazed.
Khazi	Toilet.
Knock seven bells out of	To give a severe beating.
Laiking	Messing around. Larking.
Lathered	Sweating.
Leaguer	To set up a camp.
Like Billy-O	Very fast.
Like blazes	Forcefully.
Like nobody's business	To a high degree.
Like the clappers	Very quickly.
Look a gift horse in the mouth	To be dismissive of something that has been given freely.
Lousey	Lice-ridden.
Malarky	Nonsense.
Mardy	Whining. Bad tempered.
Mash	Brew up tea.
Mukka	Friend.
Miadan	Bengali for "open field." The British Army also used it to refer to a parade ground.

Middlin'	Unexceptional. Not bad.
Month of Sundays	A long time.
More on its plate	Other things occupying its time or energy.
Mucking about	Spending time doing useless activities.
NAAFI	Navy, Army, Air Force Institute. Used mainly to refer to mobile canteens.
Nesh	Weak, delicate, feeble.
Nippy	Cold.
Not by a long chalk	Not by any means.
Not on your Nelly	Certainly not.
Nowt	Nothing.
Owt	Anything.
On the trot	Consecutively.
Palaver	Unnecessarily complex, or time-consuming procedure.
Pie-eyed	Drunk. Intoxicated.
Piquet	A Guard.
Played like a fiddle	Skilfully manipulated.
Pleased as Punch	Delighted. Phrase originates from British street entertainment featuring a puppet called Punch.
Potcheen	Home-distilled Irish whiskey.
Pretty penny	A lot of money.
Puddin' burner	Someone who would not make a good wife.
Pugari	Afghan turban.
Puking-up	Vomiting.
RASC	Royal Army Service Corps.

Glossary

Reight	Right.
Ruering	Weeping uncontrollably.
Rum	Strange.
Sam Brownes	Military belts that have a shoulder strap.
Sappers	Royal Engineers.
Scarborough warning	Advice of extreme punishment if rules are infringed.
Shellacking	Severe verbal warning, or physical punishment.
Shift	Move.
Smashing	Wonderful.
Snap	Food.
Sod	An irritating, sneaky person.
Soddin'	An exclamation used to express extreme frustration or anger *mind his own soddin' business!"*
Soft Mick	An expression indicating an abundance of something. *"He's had more accidents than Soft Mick."*
Spuds	Potatoes.
Starkers	Naked.
Summat	Something.
Swan around	To amble about, carelessly.
Sweet Fanny Adams	Nothing.
Tab-hanging	Listening without permission.
Tad	A small and insignificant amount.
Tear-arsed	Moved rapidly.

Tha	You, or your. *"Where tha going?" "Mind tha manners."*
Thissen	Yourself.
Til the cows come home	For an indefinite period.
Titfers	Hats.
Tizzy	A state of nervous excitement or agitation.
To-do	Angry exchange.
Took a shine to	Attracted to, romantically.
Traipsing	Walking carelessly, needlessly.
U-boats	German submarines. In the Mediterranean, the term was also used by the British, to include Italian submarines.
Umpteenth	Used to emphasize that something has happened many times. *"That's the umpteenth time that has happened."*
Up the creek	In trouble.
Vichy	Term for the collaborationist government of France.
Wadi	(Arabic) A ravine that is dry except in the rainy season.
Wagging it	Taking absence without leave.
Wallah	(Hindi) A person employed in a particular activity. *"A kitchen wallah." "An office wallah."*
Warm'un	A witty person. A slapper (female) *"She's a bit of a warm'un."*
Wazzock	A stupid, or annoying person.
Willies	A nervous feeling.
Zig-zig	French expression for copulation.

Remembrance

The Mauley Window in the South Nave of York Minster bears the following inscription:

"This window was restored by an old officer of the Regiment in memory of the officers, NCOs, and men of the QO Yorkshire Dragoons who fell during the Great War 1914-1918. It was removed for safety November 1939 and replaced by the Regiment in 1948 as a tribute to all Yorkshire Dragoons who gave their lives in the war of 1939-45."